Records
of the Life

of the

Venerable
Master
Hsüan Hua

THE FORTY-FIFTH PATRIARCH FROM ŚAKYAMUNI BUDDHA
THE EIGHTEENTH PATRIARCH IN CHINA FROM BODHIDHARMA
THE NINTH PATRIARCH OF THE WEI YANG LINEAGE
THE FIRST PATRIARCH IN THE WEST
DHYĀNA MASTER HSÜAN HUA （宣化 禪師）

Records of the Life
of the

Venerable Master Hsüan Hua

Volume One

Compiled and translated by
American Bhikshuni Heng Yin

Dharma Realm Buddhist University
Buddhist Text Translation Society
Talmage, California   1981

RECORDS OF THE LIFE

of the

VENERABLE MASTER HSÜAN HUA

VOLUME I

Copyright (c) by the Sino-American Buddhist
Association, Inc.

Printed in the United States of America

First printing: October 11, 1973, Sixteenth Day
                 of the Ninth Lunar Month,
                 The Anniversary of the Day the
                 Master Left the Home-Life
Second printing: July 20, 1981, Anniversary of
                 Kuan Yin Bodhisattva's Accomplish-
                 ment of the Way

ISBN 0-917512-78-2

For information, address:

    The Sino-American Buddhist Association
    Gold Mountain Monastery
    1731 15th Street
    San Francisco, Ca. 94103

ACKNOWLEDGMENTS

     This work presents the remarkable and signi-
ficant events in the life of the Venerable Master
Hsuan Hua. It has been compiled primarily from
records made by the Venerable Master's disciples
from all over the world, although other sources
have been consulted wherever available. Among these
are included the Chinese editions of his life, as
well as newspaper accounts, transcripts of instruc-
tional talks, tape transcripts, and students' notes.
     The entire work, when complete, will consist
of three volumes: the first covers the Master's
early years in China up until the time he received
the Dharma transmission from the Venerable Hsu Yun;
the second volume will be concerned primarily with
his life in Hong Kong; and the third will consider
 the period which begins with his arrival in America. Volume One has been compiled over a period of
five years by sifting through all available material, and then translating, writing, editing,
and arranging it.
     Of those assisting in the work, acknowledg-
ments are made first of all to Upāsaka Kuo Chiao,
compiler of the Chinese edition, *Tu Lun Fa Shih Shih
Chi*, *"The Biography of Dharma Master Tu Lun,"* as well as
to Bhikṣu Heng Ting who revised that work. Ack-
nowledgment is also due to Upāsakā Kuo Tak as re-
porter and Upāsaka Kuo Chen, M.A., and Upāsika Tan
Kuo Cheng as translators of the English edition,
The Remarkable Events of Dhyāna Master Tu Lun.
     Many thanks are due to Bhiksu Heng Kuan, M.A.,
for his painstaking work in editing and preparing
the volume for press, and to Bhikṣu Heng Yo, B.A.,
for assistance with the photographs and layout.
     Thanks are due to Bhikṣunī Heng Ch'ih, who
is now working on the second volume, for help in
all stages of preparation of material and for editorial assistance. For her careful editing and
helpful suggestions, thanks are also due to Bhik-
sunī Heng Hsien, Ph.D.
     Thanks are given, also, to Upāsakas I Kuo
Jung, M.A., and Kuo Yu Lineburger, B.A., and to
Upāsaka Kuo Chou Rounds, A.B., for their sound
editorial advice.
     Acknowledgements are made as well to Upāsikā
Kuo Chin Vickers for editorial assistance and advice, to Upāsikās Kuo Sui Goldstein, M.A., and
Kuo Yu Seeley, for their help in reading the

proofs, and to Upāsikā Kuo Ta Passage, B.A., for
the cover design.

We are especially grateful to Upāsika Hsia
Ping-Ying, Professor of Chinese Literature and
Composition and well-known author and scholar, for
her extensive help with the technicalities of the
Chinese. Thanks are also due to Upāsaka Lee Kuo
Ch'ien and Upāsaka Kuo I Foorman for their help in
printing the volume.

There are many others who decidedly deserve
mention for their assistance--literary, financial,
and critical--but because of space limitation they
cannot all be named here.

As the Master's disciples, it is our wish that
all who read the work will be inspired to bring
forth the heart of Bodhi. May all the merit ac-
crued be transferred to all the living beings of
the Dharma Realm so that together we may leave
suffering and attain bliss.

Disciple Bhikṣuṇī Heng Yin,
American Citizen
October 1, 1973

TABLE OF CONTENTS

Records of the Life of Dhyāna Master Hsuan Hua:
Cover Calligraphy by painter Upāsaka Chang Dai-chien;
Calligraphed title page by Professor Tseng Hsien-pin.

題宣化事迹

宣不可宣
化無所化
光影幻事
虛空鳥迹

印順 題

For the biography of Master Hsuan Hua,

Proclaiming that which cannot be proclaimed,
Teaching that which cannot be taught,
The work, an illusion--light and shadow--
As the tracks of a bird in empty space.

Written by Yin Hsun

人間生佛

石齋居士敬題

A Buddha born among mankind--

Respectfully written by
Upāsaka Shih Chi

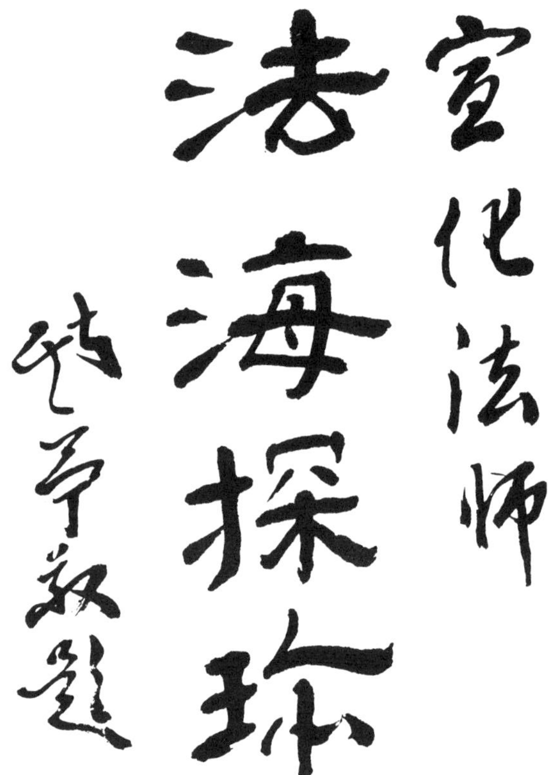

Dharma Master Hsuan Hua, who

from the sea of Dharma gathers jewels--

Respectfully written by Nan T'ing

From left to right: Miss Ananda Jennings, the Venerable
Master Hsu Yun, and the Venerable Master Hsuan Hua.

_In the winter of 1948, American Buddhist disciple
Miss Ananda Jennings, having long admired the lofty virtue
of the Venerable Master Hsu Yun, made the long and arduous
journey to Nan Hua Monastery to take refuge with Master Hsu
Yun and to attend a seven-day Ch'an meditation session.
The above picture was taken on the final day of the session.
Master Hsuan Hua was at that time acting as Head of the
Vinaya Academy.

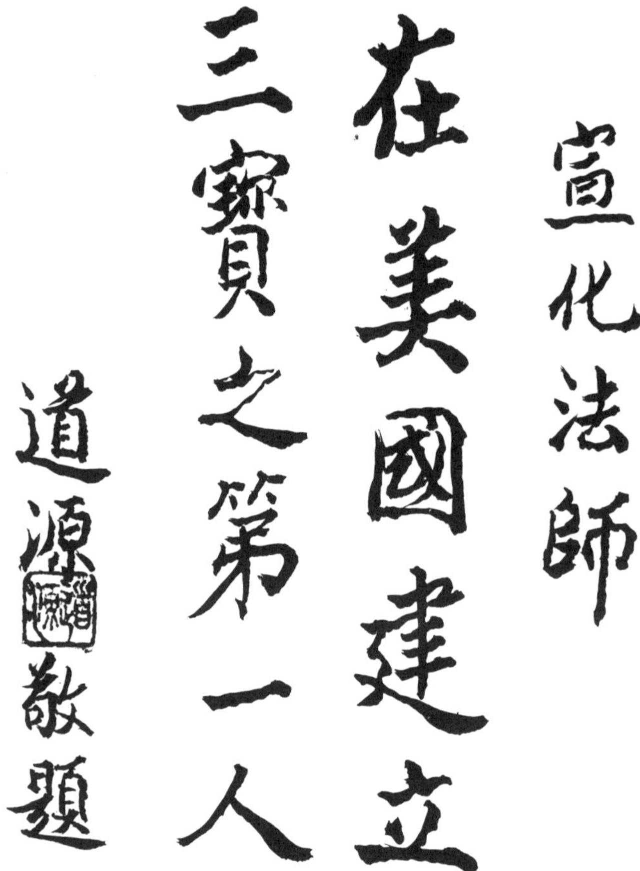

Dharma Master Hsuan Hua, who is

the first person to establish the Triple Jewel in
America

Respectfully written by Tao Yuan

Dhyāna Master Tu Lun

The Venerable Master Hsuan Hua
as a young cultivator.

Great Master Hsuan Hua

A Vast Covering: The Dharma Rain.

Respectfully written by
Tsang Kuang En, Ph.D.
Professor of Literature,
San-gyō University
Kyōto, Japan

TRANSLATOR'S INTRODUCTION

Through the power of his vows and great compassion, the Venerable Master Hua has come to transmit the Orthodox Buddhadharma to the Western world. Before leaving China for Hong Kong, and then for the United States, the Master served as Dean of the Vinaya Academy at Nan Hua Monastery, where he received the Dharma transmission from the Venerable Master Hsu Yun. Thus, the Master is the Forty-fifth Patriarch from Śākyamuni Buddha, the Eighteenth Patriarch in China, the Ninth Patriarch of the Wei Yang Lineage, and the First Patriarch in the West.

Although there are many who claim that this is the Dharma-ending age, the Master upholds and propogates the Orthodox Dharma and has founded Gold Mountain Monastery in San Francisco, where that Dharma is taught and practiced. The Master has held Dharma assemblies on the *Śūraṅgama Sūtra*, the *Lotus Sūtra*, the *Diamond Sūtra*, the *Heart Sūtra*, and others and is currently lecturing the *Great Avataṃsaka Sutra*. The four-fold assembly of disciples listens, considers, and cultivates accordingly.

On Chinese New Year's day, 1968, the Master announced to a group of listeners, "This year the Dharma Flower will bloom in America--a five-petalled flower." That summer, a group of students gathered to attend a 96-day *Śūraṅgama Sūtra* Study and Cultivation Session. In the fall of the following year, five of the students travelled to Keelung, Taiwan, to receive the Full Three Platforms of Precepts-- Srāmaṇera, Bhikṣu, and Bodhisattva Precepts, and returned as the first properly ordained American Bhikṣus and Bhikṣunīs.

In the summer of 1972, under the Master's guidance, the Three Platforms of Precepts were transmitted for the first time on Western soil, at Gold Mountain Monastery, and Buddhism became self-perpetuating in the West.

The Master has said, "I have come to America to create Patriarchs, to create Buddhas, and to create Bodhisattvas." To this end, and to counteract the declining standards of Buddhist practice in the East, the Master has instituted the Gold Mountain Doctrine, which his disciples reverently uphold:

The Gold Mountain Doctrine

Freezing, we do not scheme.
Starving, we do not beg.
Dying of poverty, we ask for nothing.
We accord with conditions, but do not change.
We do not change and yet accord with conditions.
These are our three great principles.

We renounce our lives to do the Buddha's work.
We shape our lives to create the ability
To make revolution in the Saṅgha order.
In our actions we understand the principles,
So that our principles are revealed in our actions.
We carry out the pulse of the Patriarch's heart-
     transmission.

Thus, we know that the Master has brought to the West the greatest of all gifts, the gift of Dharma. Having planted it firmly on Western soil, it may now take root, flourish, and bear the fruit of enlightenment, bringing inconceivable benefit to all living beings, and causing the Dharma to dwell in the world. For this, we are truly grateful.

Bhikṣunī Heng Yin, American Disciple
San Francisco, Buddha's Birthday, 3000
May 10, 1973

COMMEMORATIVE INTRODUCTIONS

Sometimes an event of such magnitude occurs to an individual that it radically alters the course of his life. For a small yet steadily increasing number of people this has been the case upon our encountering the Elder Tripitaka Master Hsüan Hua. Due to the karmic matrix, perhaps there were some of us who wished to do away with the violence, enmity and suffering which characterize this world; or some who wanted to find some sort of ultimate True Freedom; or some who had hit a low point on a cycle of self-injurious actions in the name of art or love. The Master has compassionately, patiently, and graphically shown us that in order to change the world, one must eliminate the origins of what makes the world violent, hateful, and painful in one's own mind; that true freedom is to be had simply by ending the cycle of birth and death; and that to harm oneself or others creates fitting retribution to be undergone in the future.

That the Master, a strictly orthodox exemplar of the ideal of all five schools of Buddhism, has been able to profoundly influence and change the lives of headstrong young Americans gives one a small idea of the perfection of his own practice and strength of his vows. When people begin to see the inconceivable and ineffable methods employed by the Master, and the responses which he evinces, they will get an inkling of the dynamic magnitude of the Buddha and his teachings.

American Disciple
Bhikṣu Heng Yo

Gold Mountain Monastery
September 1973

***

The Venerable High Master Hua teaches the Middle Way, which is in short, on the part of an enlightened master, the blending of true principle with expedient means, and is on the part of a student, the ability to maintain a detached but vigorous balance in his cultivation of the Way while constantly faced with a world of dualities. The adherence to the Mean followed by both master and disciples, extends throughout the various stages of cultivation and attainment on the orthodox path

to enlightenment. Thus the Venerable Master Hua
teaches that spiritual penetrations such as knowledge of past lives, knowledge of others' thoughts,
the ability to heal, and the like, are to be regarded as incidental to the final goal of cultiva-
tion--Buddhahood, total enlightenment. Although
such powers are not to be regarded as an end in
themselves, they provide effective tools for the
sage firmly rooted in the Middle Way who is intent
upon teaching and transforming others.

The records of miracles performed by the Venerable Master which are contained in this volume
are testimony to the Master's unsurpassed wisdom
in the use of expedient means, as well as an af-
firmation of his unceasing compassion which extends
not only to human-kind but also to beings who have
wandered off the Middle Way into deviant and demonic states. The *Suraṅgama Mantra*, as revealed in
the *Suraṅgama Sūtra*, and the *Great Compassion Mantra*, as
revealed in the *Great Compassion Heart Dhāraṇī Sūtra*, are
two important Dharmas which the Master propogates.
As long as there are disciples of the Buddha who
are able to hold these mantras and accord with the
principles of the Middle Way, then even the fier-
cest deviant and demonic beings can be led from
the hells they are creating.

Thus it is with the hope of awakening the faith
of all beings and encouraging the study and practice of the Buddhadharma that this *Records of the
Life of the Venerable Master Hsuan Hua* is presented.

American Disciple
Bhikṣuṇī Heng Ch'ih

***

The Venerable Master Hsuan Hua was writing
characters for the Chinese lesson on the black-
board late one afternoon when I very quietly realized that everything the Master does is perfect.
I had had no particular doubts before and had been
the Master's disciple for a long time, wanting nothing more than to receive the Bhikṣuṇī precepts
from him and leave home--which I later was to do.
But I had not been fully aware of his state until
that time. The sudden insight was not an intel-
lectual undorstanding based on proof, nor was it
the result of an emotional commitment to belief.
It was simply on a small scale what the *Avataṃsaka*

Sūtra calls "obtaining a door to liberation," a
tiny chink in the wall of ignorance through which
one views the magnitude of the Buddha's realm.
For I'm fully convinced, know beyond a doubt, that
the Master's mind is identical with the mind of all
Buddhas, and that each of his actions is totally
devoid of self. His every move accords completely
with what each living being needs to be taught to
gain enlightenment, and that is the total reason
for his being.

How people can follow lesser teachers who
make mistakes and still have selfish desires I no
longer understand. But I do remember what it was
like to be searching desperately for someone to
tell me something about how to leave confusion,
get a hold of myself, and become free. Most people out of desperation talk themselves into believ-
ing in someone who knows only a little more than
they, or who pretends he does. The Master makes
no pretenses. He will even tell you, "Don't believe in me!" That is, don't use your common person's mind to construct a belief-structure which
you then accept or reject--giving yourself a lot
of work when there is no work to do. Don't try to
add belief to your basic recognition of the Buddha's state.

The Master also means, don't believe in the
individual manifestation of a personal teacher and
attach to it as ultimate and real. The wonderful
existence of the Master derives solely from true
emptiness. This is far from anything remotely re-
sembling a cult of personality.

The world today proliferates with gurus. To
most you pay your fee and they take you to a heaven (or hell) which they term "complete Enlightenment." But such teachers are not devoid of self
and so they form part of the conditioned world,
and are consequently subject to production, dwelling, decaying, and extinction. That is, they are
not free. The Master is totally devoid of self
and therefore totally free. For this reason he
does not even seek disciples--how much the less
their fees. For he has reached a realm in which
there is nothing more to seek, and in which all
beings are seen as Buddhas, as I understand that
state. Yet this is coupled with inconceivably
vast vows to rescue every single living being, and
not to attain unsurpassed, perfect, right Enlight-
ment before each one does. Through the power of

his vows he already is Master to each one of us, and doesn't have to seek us out. But if we sincerely from within the prison of a limited, individual realm personally seek his aid, he will not fail to respond and lead us quickly to Buddhahood.

Bhikṣuṇī Heng Hsien
American Disciple

***

When the sun shines on one side of the world, there is darkness on the other side. Night falls on the east as day breaks in the west. The light of the Buddha's wisdom is beyond all opposites and can shine over the entire universe. Now the light of the Buddha has begun to dawn in the West, and promises light to all the world. How is this coming about?

Bodhidharma, the 28th Patriarch of Buddhism in India, saw that the great vehicle roots in China were ripe. Thereupon he took the Buddha's mind seal from India to China, thus becoming the first Chinese Patriarch. He carried on the orthodox transmission of the Dharma Eye Treasury which has been transmitted heart-to-heart from the time of Sākyamuni Buddha to each generational Patriarch.

The transmission has continued unbroken and is still in the world. It has now been brought to America by the 18th Patriarch in China, the 45th Patriarch from Sakyamuni Buddha, the 9th Patriarch of the Wei Yang Lineage, and the First American Patriarch, the Venerable Master Hua.

The Master has come from China with the Orthodox Dharma Treasury, the true and proper Buddhadharma. His vast compassion for all beings has brought him into this realm of suffering so that we who are caught in the wheel of rebirth might know the world-transcending dharma. Those who heed his inconceivable teaching can find the true path of cultivation whereby complete liberation is reached.

Such a perfectly enlightened sage rarely appears in the world. The Master's every action and word is for the purpose of enlightening and saving living beings. We are very lucky indeed to have met the Master and should not miss this opportunity to draw near to him. It may be many aeons before we again have the opportunity to work out our own liberation under the guidance of one who has crossed over and come back again.

The example set for us by the Master in his conduct, speech, and wisdom is so awesome and selfless, so pure, and so perfect that we cannot help but know that he appears in the world only because of infinitely compassionate vows to guide living beings toward the light, in this age of deepening darkness. The light which he brings is brighter than that of the sun, moon, and stars put together, because it is the source of all light, the pure bright Buddhanature which is inherent in all of us.

American Disciple
Upāsīka Kuo Chin Vickers

***

The news that there is after all a way out of the suffering and difficulties that beset us in life is the import of this book. It is actually news to us in the West, because our experience of "ways out" has, for almost all of us, been really no experience at all, but merely conjecture about a God and an afterlife and a moral order, conjecture which we have either strained to believe or just rejected as preposterous or useless. But recounted in this book, and in the volumes that are to follow, is the life of a man who does not conjecture, but who has experienced in his own life what it means to be free, and who has followed the way out to its end, where he has found the answers to the ultimate questions.

Buddhism is full of wonders, as this book shows. But in Buddhism the wonders are matter-of-fact. There is more to life than meets the eye, as all but the blindest of us suspect; and in that realm of the invisible lies freedom and great powers and great clarity; but the mysteriousness of truth rests not in the truth itself but in our own ignorance of it. Dharma Master Hsuan Hua is not a practicer of the occult and the mysterious; it is simply that he knows about the invisible, because he has seen it. He has mastered it, and he teaches us what he and the numberless others besides him in the past have learned about it so that we, too, may learn, in time and with sufficient diligence, to master it ourselves.

There is really nothing to compel Master
Hsuan Hua to teach us what he knows. People who
have mastered life do not have to waste time in
its embroilments. But as he did in China as recounted in this volume, so now he continues in
America to push and pull and cajole and inspire
and patiently explain and compassionately heal so
that his many disciples can work their way toward
enlightenment.

You who read this book are lucky, just as I
am, to be learning of this Dharma Master. So
seize the day!

American Disciple
Upāsaka Kuo Chou Rounds
September, 1973

***

The Elder Dharma Master Hsuan Hua
    as I know him . . .

Upāsikā Hsia Ping-Ying
translated by
Bhikṣunī Heng Ch'ih
American Citizen

I first came to Gold Mountain Monastery and
heard the Elder Dharma Master's instruction on
April 23, 1973. Since then, about a year and five
months have passed. During this short time I visited the Monastery once a week whenever I could, or
when I had more time I came two or three times a
week to hear the Elder Dharma Master lecture the
Sūtras and to join the assembly in bowing to the
Buddha. I have believed in Buddhism and have taken refuge as a disciple in the Triple Jewel for
nearly twenty years, but frankly speaking, I have
been formally introduced to bowing to the Buddha
and listening to Sūtras only since I came to Gold
Mountain Monastery.

By way of introduction, several years ago my
very good friend, Upāsikā I Chun said, "The Monk
in the Grave is an unusual Master. The people he
does not wish to see, he simply does not see, and
if perchance he should meet them, he doesn't talk
to them. Looking at him, you'd think he lacked
eloquence, when in actuality he reflects the Great
Wisdom which is like Stupidity." Outwardly, he is

an extremely stern and distant person. But he
truly has the heart of a Bodhisattva, and constantly helps those who are in need of help, whether
they are Buddhists or not. He views everyone with
the same kindness.

The Master often says, "There is only one Buddhadharma. Its nature is universal. There isn't
any Indian Buddhism, Chinese Buddhism, Thai Buddhism, or Japanese Buddhism. According to the Buddhadharma, the entire world consists of just one
family, and should be united rather than divided
by distinctions."

The Elder Master greatly approves of all those
who carry on the work of constructing Buddhist
schools and the like, and all the various compassionate good works done by Dharma Masters, Upāsa-
kas and Upāsikās. In coming to America the Master
himself has resolved to rescue and teach Westerners, causing the Buddhadharma to take root in the
West so that it can flourish and spread everywhere.
To date, English translations of the *Sixth Patriarch
Sūtra* and *The Heart Sūtra* have been printed, and the
Lotus Sutra and the *Earth Store Bodhisattva Sūtra* are
about to be printed. Eight other Sūtras are being
prepared for publication in the near future. Such
great work has limitless merit and virtue.

The thirteen men and women members of the
Saṅgha of Gold Mountain Monastery who are under the
leadership of the Elder Master never relax their
bitter cultivation day or night. They work all
the time. If the Elder Master did not conduct himself in a similar manner, I believe that such ac-
complishments would never have been realized. It
is something that I have personally witnessed. The
Elder Master's life-style is exactly the same as
his disciples: he eats one meal a day, at night he
sits in meditation, and he rises at 3:30 a.m. to
recite Sūtras.

What is different is that he prefers to take
a city bus because he does not wish to take his
disciples away from their studies and work to drive
him somewhere in the car. But if a Dharma Master
visits or if a layman needs to use the car, he
will send one of his disciples for them, help them
conduct their business, and take them home. For
instance, I, this lame one, have bothered them en-
tirely too much. I will always remember what they
have done for me and I am deeply grateful.

The Elder Master's Sutra lectures are also unique. After he finishes lecturing a passage of text, he will ask the disciples in the assembly, "Is there anything which you don't understand? Is there any place where I have lectured incorrectly? Please don't stand on ceremony. Speak up and we'll investigate it together." That's how open-minded, honest, and unassuming he is. Often the disciples do have questions and there are discussions. That is the open and democratic atmosphere he provides.

Currently, the Dharma Masters at Gold Mountain Monastery are busily preparing to conduct ceremonies to formally install an image of a Thousand-Armed Avalokitesvara Bodhisattva, an offering which recently arrived from Hong Kong. At the same time they will hold the opening ceremonies for the International Institute for the Translation of Buddhist Texts which is located in San Francisco at 3636 Washington Street.

And one more thing: the young Dharma Masters have completed a translation of the Elder Master's biography into English and have readied it for publication so that Westerners can come to know the rare flavor of Dharma and establish an affinity with the Buddha. They have asked me to write a little about my impressions of the Elder Master. To tell the truth, the depth of the Elder Master's scholarship, Way-Virtue, cultivation, and propagation of the Tripiṭaka is something which such an insignificant person as I cannot describe; I take inadequate pen in hand to write one ten thousandth part of it.

The Master says, "I am a simple person and don't equal others. In my eyes and heart everyone is better than me. My greatest hope is that all my disciples are better than me."

He also often says, "I want to nourish new blood for the Buddhadharma. The world belongs to young people.

"On the other hand I think that old people have a wealth of experience and young people have the strength of courage and vigor. In this society it is essential that the old and young work together so they can build a beautiful and full existence based on the ideal of the Land of Ultimate Bliss!"

September, 1973

                    FOREWORD TO THE LIFE
                 A Biographical Sketch of
            Dhyāna Master Hsuan Hua (宣化)

     The Ninth Patriarch of the Wei Yang Lineage
is Tripitaka Master Hsuan Hua of Gold Mountain
(金山). His name means "Proclaim and Transform,"
a fitting appellation for one destined to transmit the proper Dharma to new soil. Dedicated to
saving the Dharma from its impending death in Asia,
and so firmly establishing it in the West, the
Master transcends the highest standards of cultivation.
     A native of Shuang Ch'eng County in Manchuria,
the Master, who is also know as An T'zu (安慈)
and Tu Lun (度輪), was born into the Pai (白)
family. The night before his birth his mother saw
Amitābha Buddha brilliantly lighting up the world,
and when she awoke her room was filled with rare
and delicate fragrances. Shortly thereafter the
Master was born. He was to become widely known
for his devoted respect and care of his parents.
     When his mother died, the Master left the
home-life at Three Conditions Temple (三緣寺),
which is just south of Harbin in Northern China.
He was nineteen. As soon as he had taken the ten
precepts of the Srāmanera he returned to live beside his mother's grave and observe the mourning
period of three years. Here he lived through the
four seasons in an A-frame hut made of sorghum
stalks and cultivated Dhyāna concentration and
recollection of the Buddha, always sitting and
never lying down. He ate one meal a day and occasionally entered Dhyāna samādhi for weeks at a
time, never rising from his seat.
     Word of the Master's cultivation spread far
and wide and the miraculous events that took place
are too numerous to relate. He freed many people
from the burdens of disease and other afflictions,
and his followers numbered in the tens of thousands.
     One night the residents of the nearby village
saw that the Master's hut was on fire. A brilliant light shot up ten yards in the air, and the
area around the hut was as bright as broad daylight.
Many rushed to the graveyard crying, "The filial
son's hut is on fire!" and soon there were hundreds of people there to lend assistance with buckets of water. When they arrived, however, they

found the hut as peaceful as before; the Master
was sitting absorbed in meditation.

On one occasion, the Sixth Patriarch, Hui
Neng of the T'ang Dynasty, came to his hut and
told him that in the future he would go to the
West. There he would meet those with whom he had
conditions and establish the proper Dharma. The
Sixth Patriarch further predicted that the Dharma
would flourish from the Master's teaching and
spread throughout the new land.

After the Second World War the Master travelled the three thousand miles to Nan Hua Monastery in Kuang-tung to pay his respects to the
Venerable Abbot Hsu Yun, who was then one hundred
and nine years of age. During his travels he re-
sided at P'u T'o Mountain to receive the complete
precepts of the Bhikṣu in 1947. When he arrived
at Nan Hua, the two masters greeted one another
and chatted,and the Venerable Master recognized
Master Hsuan Hua to be a worthy vessel for the
propogation of Dharma, sealed and certified his
spiritual skill, and transmitted the wonderful
mind seal to him. He then asked the Master Hsuan
Hua to serve as the head of the Nan Hua Academy
for the Study of the Vinaya. The Master Hsuan Hua
wrote a gāthā describing their meeting:

> When the Noble Yun saw me he said,
>   'Thus it is.'
> I saw the Noble Yun and certified
>   this Suchness.
> The Noble Yun and I were Thus,,
> And hoped that every living being
> In the Universe would be Thus too.

In 1949 he resigned his post at Nan Hua and
went to Hong Kong where he lived in Kuan Yin Cave
on a mountainside. He only left his retreat when
he saw that it was necessary to help provide refuge for the thousands of saṅgha members who had
fled from the civil strife on the mainland.

While in Hong Kong, the Master lectured Sūtras and built Bodhimandas.   In 1951, the Master built Hsi Le Yuan Temple (西樂園寺). In 1954,
he built Tz'u Hsing Dhyāna Monastery (慈興禪寺),
and shortly after that he established the Hong
Kong Buddhist Lecture Hall (佛敎講堂).

In 1958 the Master's disciples in America
founded the San Francisco Buddhist Lecture Hall

(　佛教講堂　）. During that year the Venerable
Master Hsu Yun fell ill and the Master conducted
the Medicine Master Repentance on his behalf.

The Venerable Master Hsu Yun died on the
twelfth day of the tenth month, 1959, and the Master immediately organized a twenty-one day Buddha-
recitation session and then conducted a one hundred and twenty day memorial session during which
the *Large Sutra on the Perfection of Wisdom* was recited.

When the body of a Buddha or sage is cremated,
one may find brilliant, solid, gem-like crystals
in the remains. They are sarīra, "body-seeds,"
and testify to the purity of the sage's conduct
and the inconceivability of his realm.

The remains of the Venerable Master Hsu Yun
contained many such sarīra. Master Hua sent his
disciples to bring them to Hong Kong for veneration. On the following pages are pictures of the
Master paying reverence to the Venerable Master
Hsu Yun's sarīra. Beneath the pictures are memorial verses composed by Master Hua along with English translations.

For details on the above, the reader is referred to Volume Two of the Master's biography.

The Master left Hong Kong after a decade to
carry the proper Dharma to the West. After he
arrived in America he waited another ten years until those with whom he had conditions came to him
to be taught and transformed. Once a disciple
asked the Master, "How have you lived all these
years?"

The Master replied, "With me it's always
'Everything's Okay.' I don't beg for food if I'm
starving; I don't scheme if I'm freezing; and I'm
not obsequious if I'm poverty-stricken."

The Master has established the proper Dharma
firmly in the West so that it can become self-
propagating and flourish. He has built a large
monastery in San Francisco, where the many people
who have come have learned to turn from evil and
practice good for the benefit of their country and
the whole world. In every instance, after establishing the Dharma, he has entrusted it to his
disciples, and has turned over all the affairs of
the Saṅgha to them, keeping nothing for himself,
so that the Dharma will have a true foundation in
America.

As a part of his selfless work to teach and
transform living beings in all the realms accord-

ing to the needs of their karma, he has spent hours every day for years explaining the major Sūtras. He has trained his disciples to translate these Sūtras and their commentaries and to explain them as well. He has held assemblies on the *Surańgama Sūtra*, the *Heart* and *Diamond Sūtras*, the *Sixth Patriarch Sūtra*, the *Amitābha Sūtra*, the *Sūtra of the Past Vows of Earth Store Bodhisattva*, the *Lotus Sutra*, and the *Great Compassion Heart Dhāranī Sūtra*. Although his gifted commentaries are directed to the needs of the the American listeners, they thoroughly elucidate these Sūtras so that their wonderful meaning is preserved within the tradition of Buddhism as it has been transmitted from Sākyamuni Buddha through Bodhidharma to the present.

Less than a handful of men every three or four centuries are capable of explaining the King of all Sūtras and the ultimate expression of the Dharma Realm, the *Avatamsaka Sūtra*. The Master Hsuan Hua is now revealing this Sūtra in all its splendor, thereby insuring that the complete teaching of Sākyamuni Buddha will come to the new world.

This is but a brief portrait of a man hailed as the most remarkable Bhiksu of this era. It is included here to provide continuity to a three-volume work of which this volume is the first, the second and third presenting the noteworthy events in the Master's life in Hong Kong and the West respectively. When completed, the work will be an invaluable record of a guardian of Enlightenment in the modern age.

Bhikṣu Heng Kuan
American Disciple

虚雲老和尚法相

The Venerable Master Hsu Yun

Verse in Praise of the Old Master's Image

The revival of the Buddha's law came from the Noble Yün,
Who also glorified the schools and the Dharma doors.
The Sangha all relied upon and drew near to him.
Thus, the Triple Jewel dwells in the world,
    reaching all beings.
'Tho I'm an unschooled mountain-dwelling Sangha
    member,
I've received in transmission the seal of the
    Wei-yang line.
"Thus it is, thus it is, and once more, it is thus."
We only pray that with kind eyes you will look on
    living beings.

Reverently composed by
Disciple-in-Dharma-transmission, Tu-lun

雲公舍利正面圖　宣化禪師拜

The Venerable Master Hua pays reverence to
the sarīra of the Venerable Master Hsu Yun

讚舍利子偈
五色繽紛堅固子
萬德煆煉滿月圓
晶瑩戒珠光灼灼
碑礫定寶色鮮鮮
琉璃慧燈照法界
般若智果化三千
蓮子大小潔如玉
戒律功德眾莊嚴
嗣法門人　宣化拜題

Verse in Praise of Master Hsu Yun's Sarīra

Five-colored in profusion are the solid seeds;
Perfectly forged, the myriad virtues, like the full moon.
Lustrous is the precept pearl, it's clear light luminous,
Like mother-of-pearl, the samadhi gem, rare in hue,
Crystal like, the wisdom lamp, shining on the Dharma
  Realm;
The fruit of Prajnā wisdom transforms the universe.
These lotus seeds, great and small, are as pure as jude--
Adornments of the collected virtues of the Vinaya.

Reverently composed by
Disciple-in-Dharma-Transmission, Hsuan Hua

Records
of the Life

of the

Venerable
Master
Hsüan Hua

PART I. EARLY YEARS

The Venerable Master Hsuan Hua, who is also called An Tz'u and Tu Lun, was born in Manchuria, Sung Chiang province, Shuang Ch'eng County, near the city of Harbin on the Sungari River. The Master's father was a farmer named Pai Fu Hai. His mother, maiden name Hu, was a devoted Buddhist who ate only pure vegetarian food and recited the Buddha's name all throughout her life. She gave birth to eight children, five sons and three daughters, of whom the Master is the youngest.

One night, in a dream, she saw Amitābha Buddha emitting brilliant light which shone throughout the world and shook heaven and earth. Startled, she awoke to find the room filled with a rare fragrance and at that moment the Master was born. He cried continuously for three days out of deep sympathy for beings who suffer in the sahā world.

SEEING DEATH

The Master was raised in a remote country village. One day when he was eleven years old he saw an infant wrapped in straw lying in the brush. Its eyes and mouth were shut, and when he called to it, it did not respond. The Master had never seen death and questioned his companions who answered, "It's dead!"

Still, he did not understand the meaning of death. When he returned home he asked his mother who said, "Everyone must die. Some die of old age, some of disease, and some in accidents. Farmers, workers, merchants, and officials, the rich as well as the poor, all must eventually die.

"But there must be a way to escape death!" said the Master.

"There is," replied a visitor. "You must cultivate the Way; that is the only method. Understand your own mind and become enlightened to your basic nature. In this way you may end birth and death and stop the revolving wheel of rebirth."

Although he was very young, the Master understood the profound principle. The visitor's words affected him deeply. Afterwards, he resolved to leave the home-life to be a Bhikṣu. When he asked his mother for permission she said, "Your wish to leave the home-life is truly rare and good, and if you have good roots, a firm will, and a great Bodhi heart, you may realize the supreme Buddha Way. I approve of your wish, which verifies my former dream, but I am old and will not live long. You should stay and serve your father and me. When we die you may leave the home-life to cultivate.

The Master respected his mother's wishes and followed her to worship the Buddha. He took excellent care of his parents, fanning them in the summer and warming their cold beds in the winter. He served them as if they were living Buddhas and became widely known as "Filial Son Pai."

GUIDED ACROSS

On the nineteenth day of the second lunar month, the Anniversary of the birth of Kuan Yin Bodhisattva, when the Master was twelve years old, he dreamed he was wandering in a vast expanse of wilderness. Suddenly he came upon a road which was gutted with holes like those of a sieve. They were deep, dark, and extremely dangerous. The Master knew that if he slipped and fell he would never get out again. He stood bewildered, unable to move forward or back. He had lost sight of his father and mother and could not find his way home. Remembering that he had not yet fulfilled his vow to leave the home-life, he grew frightened and began to cry, calling for the Buddha's protection.

Just then an old woman appeared wearing a patchwork robe and a string of beads. On her feet were straw sandals and in her hand a bamboo pole. Her eyes shone with a spiritual radiance and her face beamed with compassion. "Child," she asked, "Why are you so upset?"

The boy brushed his tears aside and said, "I'm lost on a dangerous road and can't find my way home."

"Don't worry," she said, "just follow me and I'll take you there."

She led him down the road. In an instant they were walking on a safe, smooth highway. He could see clearly into the distance and was free to ramble in the Dharma Realm. Seeing his home ahead, he felt a joy for which there is no name. Glancing back on the dangerous road, he saw many people following him--old and young, men and women, monks and scholars. "Who are those people?" he asked. "Where did they come from and where are they going?"

"They have an affinity with you," she said, "and they also want to go home. You must guide them well and show them the Way so that they may all arrive at Nirvāṇa. I have important work to do elsewhere, and so I shall leave you now, but soon we shall meet again."

The Master asked her name and where she lived. "You will find out when you arrive home," she said. "There's no need to ask so many questions." Suddenly she whirled around and disappeared. The Master led the people safely home and woke from his dream feeling extremely happy.

FILIAL PIETY

Filiality is the foremost of the ten thousand virtues and the foundation of all cultivation.

When the Master was very young, his ambition was to become emperor. He ordered all the village children to pile up a mound of dirt in an empty field and he sat on top of it and issued commands. Twenty, thirty, sometimes even fifty little children would silently obey. He told them to bow to him and they put their heads on the ground. But after the Master saw the dead child, his conduct changed. He no longer wanted people to bow to him, he wished to bow to them instead.

At the age of twelve, he decided to bow to his parents every day. But then he thought, "If I suddenly start bowing they might not like it and order me to stop. Everyone bows to his parents and elders at New Year's, but no one bows every day. There's no precedent for it. What shall I do?"

Then he thought of a plan:

The first time he bowed, his father was shocked. "What are you doing?" he demanded.

"I have been unfilial in the past," said the
Master, "but now I want to cultivate the Way and
put an end to birth and death. In order to cultivate it is absolutely necessary to respect one's
parents."

"You don't have to bow," said his father. "It
will be enough just to listen to us and do what
you are told."

Then the Master fabricated a vision in order
to persuade his parents to allow him to practice
filial piety. "Father," he said, "last night I
had a dream. I don't know whether it was a Buddha
or a Bodhisattva, but someone said to me, 'Your
offense karma is extremely heavy and you will soon
die unless you bow to your parents every day.'
Now, Father, I don't exactly believe the dream,
but on the other hand I certainly don't want to
die, and so I am going to bow to you."

Hearing that, his parents made no further ob-
jections. Although they didn't like it a first,
gradually they were pleased to see their son changing his habits and growing in wisdom and virtue.

FEARING NO DIFFICULTY

The Master bowed to his father and mother
three times each, in the morning and the evening--
twelve bows every day. Then he thought, "The world
is bigger than just my father and mother," and he
began to bow to the heavens, to the earth, to the
Emperor, and to his teachers as well. He also
bowed to his master, even though he had not yet
met him. The Master knew that without the aid of
a good knowing advisor, it is impossible to cultivate, and he felt that he would meet his master
soon. He also bowed to the Buddhas, Bodhisattvas,
Pratyeka Buddhas, and Arhats, and to all the good
people in the world to thank them for all the good
deeds they had done; he bowed on behalf of the
people they had helped.

"Evil people are to be pitied," he thought,
and he bowed for them, asking that their karmic
offenses might be lessened and that they might
learn to repent and reform. When doing this, he
thought of himself as the very worst offender.
Each day he thought of new people to bow for and

soon he was bowing 837 times in the morning and 837 times in the evening, which took about three hours a day in all.

The Master didn't let others see him bow. He rose at four in the morning, washed his face, went outside, lit a stick of incense, and bowed, regardless of the weather. If there was snow on the ground, he would just bow in the snow. In the evening, long after everyone was asleep, he went outside and bowed again. He practiced this way for many years until later, while practicing filial piety beside his mother's grave, he lessened his bows to nine a day in order to save time.

Most people would not understand why he undertook such a difficult practice, but the Master has vowed to take upon himself the suffering of all beings, and fears no hardship. He has said that he would visit the hells in order to save living beings. When he was reciting the *Earth Store Bodhisattva Sutra* every day he knelt, without cushions in the brick courtyard. He knelt and recited until his knees broke open and bled, and yet it never occurred to him to stop kneeling or to bandage his knees. They healed quickly on their own.

"The more you fear suffering," the Master has said, "the more suffering you will have. Good fortune is like a bank account; accumulated good deeds make a store of blessings, but if you just spend your blessings by enjoying them, soon you will have none. To undergo suffering is to end suffering, for suffering which is endured with courage will never have to be endured again. In my life I have suffered greatly and so I wish to undergo more suffering."

This is a subtle, wonderful principle. We should investigate it in detail.

PART II. EARLY CULTIVATION

The Master continually thought, "Birth and
death is a serious problem. Death comes quickly
and the wheel of rebirth turns upon a dangerous
road. Having lost a human body, in tens of thousands of aeons it is hard to be reborn again as a
human being."
When he was twelve, the Master understood
what few are able to understand in an entire life-
time, and then only when they are old: the cycle
of becoming, dwelling, decay, and emptiness, and
the impermanence of the body of flesh. He decided
to take refuge in the Buddhadharma, and having
gained his parents' permission, set out on a pilgrimage. Visiting and talking with countless
Dharma Masters, he hoped to find a true Good Knowing Advisor.
Three years passed and he met the High Master
Ch'ang Chih. The moment he saw him he felt an affinity, as if they had been together in previous
lives. "Great Virtuous One," the Master asked,
"I beg you to teach me how to end birth and death."
The High Master Ch'ang Chih replied, "Work
hard. You must walk every step of the Way with a
firm tread. Practice with diligence. That is the
highest vehicle."
The Master was overjoyed at the instruction
and bowed to Master Ch'ang Chih as his teacher.
He took refuge with the Triple Jewel: the Buddha,
Dharma, and Sangha. He then investigated the
principles of dhyāna meditation and sought to become enlightened to the mind ground.
Great Master Ch'ang Chih was one of inconceivably high virtue and spiritual attainment. Although he had never learned to read or write, his
followers often heard him compose orally, speaking
in fluent classical prose and verse. He was able

to do so because his self-nature was open and pure
and his mind was enlightened. No matter how far
apart Master Ch'ang Chih and the Master were, Master Ch'ang Chih always knew what his disciple was
doing and the disciple knew the same of his Master.

SCHOOLING

The Master entered private school at the late
age of fifteen and was at first slow to learn. After grasping the Principles in *The Great Learning*,
however, he surpassed his schoolmates and could recite a work from memory after reading it only once.
In less than two and a half years he thoroughly
mastered the Four Books and the Five Classics and
studied the works on medicine, divination, astro-
logy, and physiognomy extensively. What he prized
most, however, were the Buddhist Sūtras.

SUDDEN AND GRADUAL

At the age of sixteen, a year after he began
school, the Master was lecturing on Buddhist Sūtras. At that time he read the *Sixth Patriarch's
Dharma Jewel Platform Sutra*, and the more he read it
the happier he became. The monks at the temple
were illiterate and had no place to go to study,
and so the Master, then a layman, stayed at the
temple and taught them the *Sixth Patriarch's Sūtra*,
the *Diamond Sūtra*, and the *Amitābha Sūtra*.
In the *Sixth Patriarch's Sūtra* we read of the
Sixth Patriarch's disciples who said, "We are the
authentic Dhyāna School, the Southern School of
Sudden Enlightenment. Our Master, the Great Master Hui Neng, is the rightful heir to the Dharma."
In the north, Shen Hsiu's disciples promoted his
Gradual Teaching saying, "All the heart-Dharma of
the Fifth Patriarch, Master Hung Jen, has been
transmitted to our teacher, Shen Hsiu." In this
way, the two schools argued back and forth.
When the Master read that he thought, "How
can there be sudden and gradual? Are they two?
Are they different?" and he wrote a couplet which
says,

> *Although sudden and gradual differ,*
> *Once complete, they are one: Why divide*
> *   north and south?*
> *Holy and common differ temporarily, but*
> *Their basic nature is the same. Don't argue*
> *   east and west.*

"Sudden" means suddenly becoming a Buddha, and "gradual" means doing it slowly. Once one has attained Buddhahood, however, there is neither "sudden" nor "gradual." Why discriminate between the Northern School of Shen Hsiu and the Southern School of the Sixth Patriarch?

It is because one has cultivated diligently and practiced the Buddhadharma in the past that one may become suddenly enlightened and reap the fruit of Buddhahood. "Holy" refers to the Buddha, and "common" refers to living beings. The two ideas seem different, but the basic nature of all living beings is the same. The Buddha is a living being who has realized Buddhahood, and living beings are Buddhas who have not yet realized Buddhahood. Sākyamuni Buddha became enlightened under the Bodhi Tree and said, "Strange, strange, strange indeed; all living beings have the Buddha nature. All can become Buddhas. It is simply because of false thinking and attachment that they do not give proof to it."

So the Master has said, "Don't say that Amitābha Buddha is in the Western Land, and that living beings in the east are simply living beings. Don't discriminate like that. The basic nature is the same, and if you truly understand the Buddhadharma, there isn't anything at all. If you debate and argue you have an attachment, and with attachments, you cannot understand the Buddhadharma.

"And don't try to promote your teacher by saying things like, 'My Master has come from China with the Orthodox Treasury, the true and proper Buddhadharma' Tell them instead that what your teacher says is empty and false. There is no Dharma which can be spoken, and there is fundamentally no right or wrong, no true or false. Don't speak of the rights and wrongs of other people. Don't be like the disciples of the Sixth Patriarch and of Shen Hsiu."

THE POWER OF GOODNESS

The Master built a free school and served as teacher. At that time an epidemic of "sheeps' hair ulcers" spread throughout the village, and eight or nine of the Master's students became infected with that painful illness. Luckily the Master knew how to take care of them, and they were soon completely healed. But then the teacher himself got sick and no one could cure him.

"Since my birth," he said, "I have dedicated my life to doing the work of the Buddhas and Bodhisattvas, and if they no longer find me of use, I shall gladly die. If they still need me, I shall be cured without medical treatment."

That night the Master woke up with a severe choking sensation in his throat. He coughed hard and spit up several lumps of "wool" and his illness was cured. From that we know the Master truly bears the responsibility for the Tathāgata's Dharma.

* * *

One day a member of the local Way Virtue Society suddenly went insane. She had been possessed by a fox spirit and her countenance and voice changed. "I am a great yellow immortal," she raged. "Because you don't pay reverence to me, I have come to punish you." The vice-president, the director, and the head lecturer all tried to reason with her, but they couldn't control her.

The Master finally stepped forward and declared, "The Way Virtue Society is established according to the decree of heaven, and in disturbing it you are contradicting heaven's will. For this reason I must now act on heaven's behalf to reprimand you. You cannot escape."

The fox spirit tried to move, but could not. Terrified, the woman knelt before the Master begging for compassion. "Let me go," the fox spirit spoke through her, "and I will never disturb the society again."

"Since you admit your error," said the Master, "you may go. If you try it again, there will be no reprieve."

The fox spirit bowed and left. It is true that heaven's law is absolutely just and can only be upheld by the virtuous.

The Master's filial conduct was respected by
all, and he was elected to succeed Sun Sheng Mao
as President of the Benevolent Society. Mr. Shao,
the Master's friend, had been the vice-president,
but he turned his back on the truth and broke the
precept against drinking liquor. Although everyone urged him to resume his position, he refused.
When the Master heard of this he said, "I will try
to persuade him to return, but if I fail, I will
kill myself and never again enter this defiled
world."
     Mr. Shao, moved by the Master's willingness
to sacrifice his very life for a friend, repented
of his error and resumed his position as before.

***

     As the head of the Way Virtue Society, the
Master not only urged others to practice the Way
but did so himself. His great virtue and selfless-
ness were admired by the entire community. He la-
bored to build free schools and meeting halls where
he lectured against alcohol, tobacco, and drugs.
He worked untiringly for the benefit of others and
never thought of himself.
     One day, beneath a tree, he read of the vir-
tuous conduct of Chang Ya Hsuan and was so impressed that he made a vow. "Heaven," he said,
"I shall certainly follow the example of Chang Ya
Hsuan."
     That very evening, a demon came to test the
Master's vow. A beautiful woman secretly entered
the Master's room and tempted him with her beauty
and with money. Caught off guard, for an instant
the Master's mind wavered, but he immediately regained his composure and thought, "She has been
sent to test my sincerity." He recited the Buddha's name, collected his thoughts, and then spoke
to the girl. "As a member of the Way Virtue Society," he said, "you should understand the principle of cause and effect. Now, would you like to
be born in heaven or would you rather go to hell?"
     "I want to go to heaven, of course," she said.
     "Then you must not act in this way," said the
Master, "because if you continue, you will certainly go to hell."
     Hearing this, she was greatly ashamed, begged
forgiveness, and left.

The Master had joined the Way Virtue Association when he was sixteen, and by the time he was seventeen he was teaching sixty to seventy men and women, many of whom were middle-aged.

In teaching, the Master always tried to simplify problems so they could be easily understood. One such problem was potato skins. Whenever a lunch was held at the Way Virtue Association, the members would not eat their potato skins.

The Master had explained about the benefits of eating what others cannot eat and of doing what others cannot do, and of how essential it is to actually put that teaching into practice. But his instruction had gone in one ear and out the other, and his students paid no attention to it at all.

One time, when the members were eating potatoes and as usual spitting the skins out on the floor until the place was littered with them, the Master took a bowl and went around picking up all the skins. Then he ate them. His students were extremely embarrassed to see their teacher eat what they themselves had chewed up and spit out. The Master's lesson on eating what others cannot eat finally had sunk in. His students repented and changed their ways.

***

When he was seventeen, the Master met an old cultivator who could sit in meditation for one or two days straight, but who was attached to his sitting. One day, the cultivator accidentally stepped on a small white mouse and killed it, and soon he went insane and could no longer enter samādhi. He asked the Master why and was told it was because he had stepped on the mouse.

"What shall I do?" the cultivator asked.

"Let him go," said the Master.

"But I don't know how," the cultivator said.

The Master did a little "work" and released the mouse. The cultivator regained his skill and once more entered samādhi. In cultivating the Way, one must be very careful.

THE DEMON OF SICKNESS

While a young student of the Buddhadharma, seventeen or eighteen years old, the Master once

had an arrogant thought: "Everyone is afraid of
demons," he said, "but I'm not. Demons are afraid
of me! Heaven demons, earth demons, god, ghost,
and human demons--I'm not afraid of any demons at
all."

Soon after he said this, a demon of sickness
came and frightened the Master. He was so sick
that he lay on his bed from morning to night, unable to eat or drink. "I spoke foolishly," he
thought, "and now a demon of sickness has found me
and there is nothing I can do."

The Master was so sick he went into a coma and
and was on the verge of death. Suddenly he saw the
three Filial Sons of the Wang Family of Manchuria.
Two of them, a Buddhist Bhikṣu and a Taoist Master,
had left the home-life, and the third was a layman.
They came and took the Master out to play. As soon
as they went out the door, their feet left the
ground and they rode the clouds and drove the wind.
They took off from the roof of the house and when
the Master looked down, the house was already very
small.

They met a lot of people and traveled everywhere, to temples, on Mt. Wu Ta'i, Mt. O Mei, Mt.
P'u T'ou and others. They also visited foreign
lands and saw people who had blond hair and blue
eyes. It was like a movie, scene after scene
quickly passed. Frame after frame, they actually
went to those places and heard those things. When
they returned, the Master opened the front door
and saw himself lying on the bed inside the house.
"How can this be?" he thought, and as soon as he
was aware that there were two of him, the two
changed into one and he opened his eyes and looked
up at his mother and father. "He's alive!" they
cried joyfully. "He's not going to die after all!"

The Master had been unconscious for six or
seven days; he hadn't eaten, drunk water, spoken,
or even opened his eyes in all that time. Having
awakened, he now knew that he had died and yet not
died. In fact, he was a living dead person, one
who had been born again. After that, he never
spoke recklessly, because he knew that if one brags
that one doesn't fear anything, something will happen to make one afraid.

EVERYTHING'S A TEST

After taking refuge with the Venerable Master Ch'ang Chih, the Master cultivated dhyāna samādhi. His skill increased day by day until he was no longer moved by external influences, whether sights or sounds. When he was eighteen years old, on the 29th day of the 12th lunar month, he had the following dream:

He dreamt he entered a three-room hut. In the southern section was a beautiful young mother with her child. She was well-dressed and extremely attractive. In the eastern section on two leather trunks stood an oil lamp. The young woman moved toward the lamp and whispered, "It's late now. You can't go back home." She glanced at him seductively and put out the light, approached the Master and embraced him.

"What are you doing? What are you doing?" shouted the Master. There was no answer and the Master thought, "She must be a demon. How else could she be so shameless?" Then he recited loudly, "Homage to the Greatly Compassionate Bodhisattva Kuan Yin. Please save me!"

With the Bodhisattva's aid, the Master awoke from his dream, but the portion of his body embraced by the demon ached for about a week.

The Master has instructed his disciples,

> *Everything's a test*
> *To see what you will do.*
> *If you don't recognize what's before*
> *   your eyes,*
> *You'll have to start anew.*

PART III: BITTER PRACTICES
         BESIDE THE GRAVE

When the Master was nineteen years old his
mother fell ill and couldn't move. He looked after her himself, changing her bedding and washing
her clothes, feeding and caring for her with filial devotion.
     Near the city of Harbin, in Pei Yin Ho, there
was a powerful creature called The Fox Immortal.
Fox immortals can transform into many kinds of beings. For example, during the Japanese invasion
of Manchuria, this particular Fox Immortal fought
the Japanese.
     The Japanese army had secretly built an elec-
trically run oil cauldron near their base, and
they shipped people in by the trainload to be
boiled in it. It was an extremely efficient opera-
tion and left no traces whatsoever.
     The Fox Immortal transformed himself into an
old man and walked into the area. The Japanese
fired their guns, but he walked right on by and
blew up the armory. Many Japanese soldiers were
killed and the rest of them moved out saying the
place was hexed.
     It was also well-known that the Fox Immortal
could cure illness. All one had to do was go to
his place, set out a bowl with a red cloth over it,
and make a request. The Master went to the Fox
Immortal seeking help for his mother. He set out
the bowl, knelt down, asked for help, and waited.
He knelt for three days and three nights without
moving, without getting up, and without eating or
drinking water, but nothing happened. At the end
of the third day he returned home and not long after that, in the third lunar month, the Master's
mother died.
     The warm spring winds had melted the winter
snow and the roads were muddy and hard to travel.

As the family burial ground was more than ten miles
away, the family and friends were worried about
how they would be able to conduct the service and
transport the coffin. The night before the funeral, the Master put in the following request, "It
would be best if the weather were cold and dry,
with a fine covering of snow on the ground for
traction." The temperature dropped, and towards
morning an inch of snow fell on the frozen ground.

About forty people attended the funeral. After the service, the sky cleared and the snow began to melt. As they started to leave, the Master
sat down beside the grave. His brothers called to
him, but he didn't answer. "The old monk has gone
into samādhi," they said, and left without him.

When the people left, trouble came. The Master sat for one day, and the next evening a large
pack of wolf dogs closed in. They were extremely
fierce and were known to eat people. The Master
thought to himself, "I'm not going to pay any attention to the dogs. Even tigers couldn't move me.
I am cultivating filial conduct for my mother, and
if the dogs eat me it will be a most honorable,
awesome sacrifice."

The dogs slunk low to the ground, snarling and
growling. From a distance of 30 feet, they inched
their way in until they were less than ten feet
from where he sat. Then suddenly the whole pack
turned and ran.

Had the Master started to run, the dogs would
have ripped him apart, but because he didn't move,
they thought, "He's not going to bother us so we
won't bother him." The dogs chased off other visitors to the grounds, but they never bothered anyone
who came to see the Master.

Some time later, after the Master had left
home, he was visiting a relative who believed in
the Fox Immortal and who had invited him to his
home to receive offerings. When the Fox Immortal
arrived and saw the Master, he immediately knelt
and begged the Master to be his teacher.

"Who are you?" the Master asked.

"I'm the Fox Immortal of Pei Yin Ho," came
the reply.

"Really?" said the Master. "I knelt for three
days seeking medicine from you, and you didn't give
it to me, and now you want me to be your teacher?
Absolutely not."

"That's not true," said the Fox Immortal. "It wasn't that I didn't want to give it to you. I wanted to create an affinity with you by giving you the medicine, but every time I approached you with it, I couldn't open my eyes. I wanted to take refuge with you even then, but I couldn't get near you."

Hearing the Fox Immortal speak that way, you may wonder just why it was that he couldn't open his eyes when he approached the Master with the medicine, but if you don't know, there is no way to explain it to you. When drawing a picture of a person, one draws the outer form, not the in-nards. In order to understand what the Fox Immortal saw, it is necessary to work hard, cultivate the Way, and figure it out for yourself.

Soon after his mother's burial, the Master went to Three Conditions Temple at P'ing Fang Station south of Harbin, and on the eighth day of the fourth lunar month, he left the home-life, receiving the ten precepts of a srāmanera, or novice monk, from the Great Master Ch'ang Chih. He then returned to his mother's grave and built a five-by-eight hut out of five inch sorghum stalks. The hut kept out the wind and rain, but there was actually little difference between the inside and the outside. Here, the Master observed the custom of filial piety by watching over his mother's grave for a period of three years. Clothed only in a rag robe, he endured the bitter Manchurian snow and the blazing summer sun. He ate one meal a day and never lay down to sleep.

At the side of the grave, the Master read many Sūtras. He first read the *Lotus Sutra* and jumped for joy. "I recited it," he said, "kneeling for seven days and nights, forgetting to sleep or eat, until blood dripped from both of my eyes ... Next, I read the *Surangama Sutra*, deeply investigating the great samādhi. Then I read the *Avatamsaka Sutra*, and my awakening was ocean-like, boundless, vast, nameless, and majestically supreme.

The Master has said,

"Cultivation is simply enduring what you cannot endure, bearing what you cannot bear. You must resolve: What others cannot do, I do. What others cannot suffer, I suffer. What others cannot eat, I eat, until the point where there is not even a thought of stealing so much as a mouthful of food or a drop of water. You say you cannot

take it? Take what you cannot take! That is cultivation, and it's the only thing that counts."

A TWENTY-THREE DAY DREAM

Since the time the Master resolved to cultivate the Way, he has eaten only one meal a day,
and that before noon. This is because he knows
that many of the world's people are hungry, and
he wishes to offer his food to them. While sitting beside his mother's grave, he did not cook
for himself, and since no one brought him food,
he simply didn't eat. Finally, a layman vowed to
bring him food every day.

When the summer rains came and the ground
was muddy, the Master told him, "I have enough
food for 20 days or so. Please don't trouble yourself to climb the steep hillside when the weather
is bad." Because he believed every word the Master said, from then on he stayed home when it
rained. Of course, the Master had not so much as
a grain of rice stored in his hut.

Once it rained for many days, but the Master
just shut his eyes to meditate and paid no attention to whether it was night or day. When the
man arrived, the Master asked, "How long has it
been since your last visit?"

"Twenty-three days," he said.

"Ah," said the Master, "I have dreamed a
twenty-three day dream."

EIGHTEEN SOLEMN VOWS

While sitting beside his mother's grave, on
the 19th day of the sixth lunar month, the Master
made the following solemn vows:

"I bow before the Buddhas of the ten directions, the Dharma of the Tripiṭaka, and the holy
Saṅgha of the past and present, praying that they
will hear and bear witness.

"I disciple Tu Lun, An Tz'u, resolve not to
seek for myself either the blessings of the gods
or of men or the attainments of the Sravakas, Pra-
tyekabuddhas, or high Bodhisattvas. Instead, I
rely on the Most Supreme Vehicle, the One Buddha
Vehicle, and bring forth the heart of Bodhi, vow-
ing that all living beings of the Dharma Realm

shall attain the Utmost Right and Perfect Enlightenment at the same time as I.
    1. I vow that I will not attain the Right En-
lightenment if there is even one Bodhisattva in the
ten directions and the three periods of time to the
end of empty space and the Dharma Realm who has not
yet become a Buddha.
    2. I vow that I will not attain the Right En-
lightenment if there is even one Pratyekabuddha in
the ten directions and the three periods of time to
the end of empty space and the Dharma Realm who has
not yet become a Buddha.
    3. I vow that I will not attain the Right En-
lightenment if there is even one Srāvaka in the ten
directions and the three periods of time to the end
of empty space and the Dharma Realm who has not yet
become a Buddha.
    4. I vow that I will not attain the Right En-
lightenment if there is even one human being in the
worlds of the ten directions who has not yet become
a Buddha.
    6. I vow that I will not attain the Right En-
lightenment if there is even one asura who has not
yet become a Buddha.
    7. I vow that I will not attain the Right En-
lightenment if there is even one animal who has not
yet become a Buddha.
    8. I vow that I will not attain the Right En-
lightenment if there is even one hungry ghost who
has not yet become a Buddha.
    9. I vow that I will not attain the Right En-
lightenment if there is even one being in the hells
who has not yet become a Buddha.
    10. I vow that I will not attain the Right En-
lightenment if there is any being in the triple
world who has taken refuge with me and has not yet
become a Buddha, be it a god, immortal, human being, or asura, a bird, fish, plant, or animal, a
magical dragon, beast, ghost, or spirit.
    11. I vow to bestow upon all living beings of
the Dharma Realm all the blessings and happiness
I am destined to receive.
    12. I vow to take upon myself the miseries of
all living beings of the Dharma Realm, that I alone
may endure them on their behalf.
    13. I vow that my spirit shall enter the hearts
of all living beings who do not believe in the Buddhadharma, causing them to reform their evil conduct
and practice the good, and causing them to take

refuge with the Triple Jewel and ultimately realize Buddhahood.

14. I vow that every living being who has seen my face or even heard my name will bring forth the Bodhi heart and quickly realize the Buddha Way.

15. I vow to observe reverently the Buddha's regulation and take only one meal a day and that at noon.

16. I vow to enlighten all living beings according to their dispositions.

17. I vow in this very life to attain the Five Eyes and the Six Spiritual Penetrations and the ability to fly freely.

18. I vow that my vows will all be fulfilled.

> *I vow to save the numberless living beings.*
> *I vow to cut off the inexhaustible afflictions.*
> *I vow to study the limitless Dharma-doors.*
> *I vow to realize the supreme Buddha-Way."*

PART IV: MIRACLES BESIDE THE GRAVE

*The twelfth of the Master's vows reads, "I
vow to take upon myself the miseries of all living
beings of the Dharma Realm that I alone may endure their suffering." In fulfilling the vow,
whenever someone sought the Master's help, he
would first determine his sincerity, and then ex-
haust his strength to help him. Since the body
is merely a temporary combination of the four
illusory elements, earth, air, fire, and water,
if one can let go of attachment to the body, any
sickness will disappear of itself. "Letting go
of attachment" means simply to set aside physical
comfort and seek instead to understand and practice the Buddhadharma for the benefit of all beings.
In this way one may learn to leave the sea of suffering and attain Nirvāṇa's permanence, purity,
true self, and bliss.*
*The incidents which follow are examples of
how the Master's Dharma power, combined with the
seeker's true sincerity, can cure any illness.*

UNUSUAL EVENTS BESIDE THE GRAVE

In the summertime the mosquitoes were big and
fierce, and although they never bit the Master, his
visitors often complained. "Why don't they bite
you?" they asked him.

"I don't know," said the Master, "I've never
really thought about it." Then he thought, "Mosquitoes have no respect for anybody. They will
bite Bodhisattvas; they will bite Arhats; they will
bite anybody, because they are really stupid.
Still, they don't bite me. Now, if the wolf-dogs
won't bite me or my guests, the mosquitoes should
leave my guests alone as well."

From then on, among the Master's visitors,

there was not one who ever got bitten by a mosquito while visiting him.

***

Once, there was a severe earthquake. The Master, sitting in meditation, simply thought, "The demon king has come to disturb my samādhi, but I am not going to move." When the quake stopped, he thought, "I have subdued the demon."

***

Another time, miraculously, the Sixth Patriarch, Great Master Hui Neng, came to chat with the Master. He told him that later the Master would go to America, described the people he would meet, and said that the Master would transmit the Orthodox Dharma to the Western World. After they had talked, the Master escorted the Sixth Patriarch out of the hut. The Sixth Patriarch took four or five steps and disappeared. It was only then that the Master remembered that the Sixth Patriarch had entered Nirvāṇa over 1200 years before.

RELIEVING THE SUFFERING OF LIVING BEINGS

When the Master was cultivating the Way beside his mother's grave, there lived in the village a woman named Chang. She had suffered from chronic vomiting for four years. Both Chinese and Western doctors were unable to cure her, and their medicines had no effect. Hearing of the Master's filial virtue, she went to the graveside, knelt respectfully, and sought help. The Master first explained to her the principles of human life in the light of the Buddhadharma, and the origin of disease as a product of cause and effect. When she had repented of her past misdeeds, he taught her to recite the name of Amitābha Buddha, which she did faithfully. She visited the Master daily and bowed to him with extreme sincerity. Within 21 days her illness was completely cured.

***

Another Mrs. Chang, who lived near P'ing Fang Station, had been paralyzed in the legs for three

years. Neither medical treatment nor sorcery had
any effect. When she heard of the Filial Son Pai,
she went by carriage to his hut and asked to be
cured.

"I know nothing about medicine," said the
Master, "and yet those who believe are healed by
virtue of their sincerity. You need only have
faith, repent of your offenses, and change for the
good. If you recite the Buddha's name and stop
eating meat, you will soon be well."

Mrs. Chang bowed to the Master and asked for
a picture of him, which she hung in her home.
Kneeling on the floor, she bowed before it daily.
After a hundred days, the paralysis disappeared
and she could move normally again. Seeing this
the entire household bowed to the Master as their
teacher. They vowed to make offerings and support
the Triple Jewel and to work energetically for the
good of mankind.

***

In Pa Chia Village, forty miles from the Master's dwelling, Tai Kuo Hsien was dying of tuberculosis. The doctors had given up hope for him,
yet he still wanted to live. He went to the Master and pleaded for his life. Seeing that he was
sincere, the Master instructed him to recite the
name of the greatly compassionate Kuan Shih Yin Bodhisattva, and to observe the precept against killing by not eating meat. Then the Master poured
water gently over his head and the sick man suddenly felt comfortable and strong. His sickness
was healed. He then took refuge with the Triple
Jewel and continued to recite the Great Compassion
Mantra and Kuan Yin's name without cease.

***

Mrs. T'ang had been in labor for four days and
was near death. Her mother-in-law went to the Master and knelt before him, crying bitterly. The
Master pitied her and said, "Return home, call the
whole family together and recite, 'Namo Kuan Shih
Yin Bodhisattva.' Then make a vow to eat vegetarian food one hundred days out of every year and
everything will be all right."

She returned home and followed the Master's
instructions. Mrs. T'ang gave birth right away

and both she and her child were safe and sound.

***

   The Master's following continued to grow in
number. In the village of Tung Ching Tzu, Wang
Feng I and his family of over thirty members all
took refuge. They were all vegetarians and worked
with great dedication to spread the Buddhadharma.
   When Wang's nephew became seriously ill, he
and the boy's father knelt before the image of the
Buddhas and Bodhisattvas and begged the Master for
help. They prayed for a full week and then one
night Wang dreamt that the Master came to his house
and gave the child a pill which the child immediately ate. When Wang awoke, he found the child
had been completely cured. Hearing this, the friends
and relatives all took refuge and cultivated together to leave the sea of suffering for the Land
of Ultimate Bliss.

THREE INS, THREE ONS

   In the Master's village lived a student named
T'ang. At age fourteen, he was stupid and sickly
and had a feeble memory. His parents and teachers
reproached him and encouraged him, but to no avail.
When he heard of the Master, T'ang and sixteen fellow schoolmates went to ask for his help in streng-
thening their wisdom and their memories. Stupid
T'ang especially wished to be a better student.
   The Master said, "Study may be classified into
two groups of three, three 'ins' and three 'ons.'
When you study, put your subject 1) in your mind,
2) in your mouth, and 3) in your eye. Do not allow any distractions to interfere. Study at all
times, 1) on the road, 2) on the pillow, and even
3) on the toilet! In general, be sincere and dili-
gent, and practice your lessons wherever you happen to be. I remember as a student I always fo-
cused my entire mind on my lessons. I saw only the
book. If an orchestra was playing next to me, I
didn't hear it. If bright colors flashed before
my eyes, I was unaware. If one can devote his entire attention to his goal, he can succeed in anything. How much the more so in study!"
   The students bowed reverently and left. After
that, T'ang's wisdom suddenly opened so greatly

that he far surpassed his schoolmates. His parents
and teachers were impressed and students flocked
from all directions to receive the Master's instructions.

TAMING A SHREW

In the village lived a woman named Yuan Mu
Hang, whom everyone called "The Tigress," for she
was unfilial to her parents-in-law, disrespectful
towards her husband, impolite to her sisters, and
rude to the neighbors.   She didn't belive in ghosts
and spirits, knew nothing of cause and effect, and
continually indulged in offensive, anti-social be-
havior. Hearing of the Master, she was curious
and went to investigate. She found him sitting
facing the West with his palms together reciting
"Namo Amitābha Buddha" without cease. Deeply impressed, she asked, "What are you doing?"
     "My parents toiled bitterly to raise me," the
Master replied, "and I wish to repay their kindness by reciting the Buddha's name so that they
may be reborn in the Western Land of Ultimate Bliss.
That is my filial duty."
     She asked further, "Is it true that, after
death, one may become a ghost?"
     The Master said, "You don't have to wait un-
til you die! If you think, speak, and act like a
ghost now, you're a ghost in this very life.
Wrathful people are red-faced ghosts and spiteful
people are yellow-faced ghosts. Those who annoy
others are white-faced ghosts, those who vex others
are green-faced ghosts and those who hate others
are black-faced ghosts. If you conduct yourself
like the five ghosts you have "five ghosts making
noise in your house," and neither you nor your
family will know any peace. You are certain, in
fact, to lose your wealth and incur all kinds of
calamities. Then, when you die, you will become
a ghost and suffer endlessly in the great hells
without escape, because you turned your back on
enlightenment and became entangled with the 'dust'
of worldly affairs. Deluded about the truth and
following the false, you bring the retribution upon yourself.
     "If you cultivate good and conquer evil, how-
ever, turning from the dust towards the truth, then
you are identical with the Buddhas, neither born

nor destined to die, neither defiled nor pure, and
neither increasing nor decreasing. Such is the im-
mutable, eternally bright reward of bliss. You
will have escaped the cycle of rebirth and ended
tens of thousands of aeons of birth and death."

Surprised and frightened, the woman began to
cry. "I never knew what it meant to be a human
being," she said, "and that one must act respon-
sibly and practice good deeds. Ignorant of cause
and effect, I have acted carelessly, but now I realize that my guilt is truly limitless and am deeply
sorry. I fear, however, that my repentance is too
late. What can I do?"

The Master said, "That you admit your former
errors is a sign that your natural goodness has
come to the fore. Your tears are of no use. Besides, people are people, not saints. Who can have
no faults at all? Your crimes may fill heaven and
earth, but if you truly repent, they are all era-
dicated. Confess openly, reform, and then consider
your past actions as if you had died yesterday and
been born again today. If, as a laywoman, you vow
to spread the Buddhadharma and encourage people to
take refuge with the Triple Jewel, your merit and
virtue will wipe those offenses away. Don't you
know that when great evil is reformed it becomes
great good, whereas one of great goodness who com-
mits offenses becomes one of great evil?"

The woman was overjoyed at the instruction,
took refuge with the Master and worked diligently
to promote the Dharma, converting over 800 people
to become his disciples. Having awakened to the
Great Vehicle, she upheld the Proper Dharma and
the villagers no longer called her "The Tigress,"
but spoke of her as "The Guiding Kuan Yin."

Towards the end of the 8th lunar month in the
autumn of 1944, she said to her relatives, "I have
redeemed my great offenses through acts of virtue.
The Buddhas and Bodhisattvas are pleased. Our Teacher, the Venerable Master, has come into the world
through the power of the great vows of Amitābha
Buddha. Believe in him! If you don't waste your
time and don't backslide you are certain to obtain
great advantage and arrive at the other shore, which
is Nirvāṇa. I have learned from the Master that
the 19th day of the 9th month is the date of my de-
departure for the Pure Land. Do not grieve, but
assist me in reciting the Buddha's name"

Her family agreed, and on the appointed day

she bathed, dressed, and sat in full lotus facing
the West. With palms together and a smile on her
face she died reciting·the Buddha's name. She was
69 years old and had eaten pure food and recited
the Buddha's name for over ten years.

THE ALLEGIANCE OF A SCHOLAR

Ku Chieh San, who had been a top-ranking Imperial scholar during the late Ch'ing dynasty, was
a man of rare literary talents and the teacher of
many well-known scholars. Although he investigated the Buddhadharma, he had been unable to grasp
its essential doctrines and so he visited the Master and requested instruction. The Master taught
him the fundamentals of dhyāna meditation, the
mind-ground Dharma-door which is not based on language.

Understanding what he had never understood before, Ku Chieh San was overjoyed. He reverently
practiced the Master's teachings and, in 1943, he
died sitting with his body in full lotus position
and his face showing a great lustre.

THE VILLAGERS SEE LIGHT

The Master's three-year mourning period was
about to expire. One evening at twilight the resi-
dents of the nearby village saw a brilliant light
ascend from the Master's hut. It rose some thirty
feet in the air, illumining the entire area as
bright as day. In alarm they cried, "The Filial
Son's hut is on fire! Is he alive or dead? We
must go put it out!" They ran to the graveyard
with buckets of water, but when they arrived they
found the tiny hut as peaceful as ever, with the
Master sitting upright by the light of a single
oil lamp, reciting the Buddha's name. In deep ad-
miration, they said among themselves that the Master had truly attained the Way as revealed through
the great beam of light.

The Master's following increased greatly from
that, and visitors came from hundreds of miles to
receive his teaching and pay their respects. Finally, when his filial duties were completed, he
went into seclusion in Amitābha Cave in the mountains east of the district. There he delved deeply

into dhyāna meditation and practiced rigorous as-
ceticism, eating only pine nuts and drinking spring
water. The area abounded with wild beasts, but
they never disturbed the Master. In fact, wolves
and bears behaved like house pets, tigers stopped
to listen to his teaching, and wild birds gathered
to hear the wonderful Dharma.

Those are all indications that the Master's
level of attainment had already gone far beyond
that which our ordinary minds can grasp and that
he had entered an inconceivable state.

STOPPING THE CYCLE

By the time he had completed the three-year
mourning period, the Master had received over 2000
visitors from all walks of life--scholars, farmers,
workers, merchants, and officials--only beggar's
were absent from the throng. Then one day Chi Ta
Fu called at the Master's hut. "Venerable Master,"
he asked, "why am I so poor?"

The Master explained to him the principle of
cause and effect. "Why is one wealthy in one's
present life? It is because one practiced giving
in lives past. Why is one poor in one's present
life? It is because one never aided the poor in
lives past."

"When I search my heart," said the beggar, "I
find no cause for shame, and yet in order to live
I must beg in the streets. If that is the result
of my past greed and selfishness, how can the cycle be stopped?"

"It is not difficult," said the Master. "You
need only sincerely believe and diligently practice and you will obtain results. Long ago there
was a man named Chu Ch'i who, understanding the
principle of the cycle of retribution, exerted himself in doing acts of virtue, and built the Shuang
Shan bridge. In his next life he was reborn in
the Imperial family and enjoyed the prosperity and
glory of a prince. Wouldn't you call that 'stopping the cycle?'"

The beggar happily bowed, took refuge, and
from that day on while begging he recited "Namo
Amitābha Buddha" without cease. Any leftover food
he always gave to the less fortunate. He practiced charity with all his might for many years,
perfecting his virtue and purifying his karma until,

in 1930, he foretold his own death, and sitting in
the lotus position facing West, he died while reciting the Buddha's name.

PART V: FROM STUDENT TO TEACHER

WONDERFUL DHARMA
One Word Makes All The
Difference
It is a New Year's custom in China to write
matched couplets. The verses are written on fes-
tive strips and displayed on both sides of the entrances to homes, businesses, and even temples.
One year, when the Master was still a novice, he
wrote the four words "Wisdom Like the Sea" as part
of a New Year's greeting.

When a fellow-novice saw the characters, he
was fascinated and began to repeat them again and
again, "Wisdom like the sea, wisdom like the sea,
wisdom like the sea..." The Master listened for
a while but finally became annoyed and said, "Your
karma is like the sea!"

The Master's words enraged the novice. He
screamed at the Master, "What do you mean, my karma is like the sea!" and he began to dance around
the Master like a boxer.

"Hey! Hey! Hey!" said the Master. "Wait a
minute. Don't get nervous. I'm going to tell you
something which is bound to please you. I said
your karma was like the sea. Instead of getting
angry, you really should thank me."

"You said my karma was like the sea," said
the novice, "and you expect me to thank you? Nothing doing."

"Let me finish explaining," said the Master.
"Do you know what karma is? It's just what people
do. There is both good and bad karma. When I
said that your karma was like the sea, I was re-
ferring to your good karma. Why are you angry?
What do you think about that?"

"Oh, no problem," said the novice, "no problem," and he invited the Master to lunch.

On another occasion, the Master, then a novice, was carrying a roll of paper when suddenly
another Dharma brother called to him, "What are

you carrying? What have you got there? Hey, you,
what's that?" He felt it his duty to make sure
that nothing got lost or wasted.
    "This?" said the Master. "It's a bill-of-
sale. You see, I just sold you, and this is the
receipt."
    The novice, who had a quick temper, was fur-
ious. "What?" he screamed. "Just what makes you
think you have the right to sell me? Who do you
think you are? What business of it is yours to
sell me?"
    "I have every right to sell you," the Master
replied, "and what is more, you're going to be
happy I did so. If it weren't going to make you
happy, I wouldn't have told you about it."
    "What right do you have...just what right..."
the novice sputtered.
    "I have the right to sell you to someone who
can make you happy," said the Master. "In fact,
I've sold you to Sākyamuni Buddha. I have done
it so that you can always be a Bhikshu."
    The novice was speechless.
    "Well," said the Master, "can I do that or
not? Are you happy now?"
    "Oh, yes, yes, you can do that," said the no-
vice. "That's all right."

BIG KNEES

    In La Lin, in the village of Pei Yin Ho, lived
Kuan Chung Hsi and his nephew Kuan Chan Hai. Kuan
Chung Hsi had been a non-Buddhist teacher, and
transmitted a dharma called "The Way of Gathering
Conditions." He told his disciples that he had
hundreds of treasures for sale at only $1,000.00
each. The treasures existed in name only, and
Kuan Chung Hsi said, "The time is not right and
so I can't give them to you now. When the time
comes, the world will change and you will have
your treasures." He had over four thousand disciples.
    When he reached fifty years of age, he rea-
lized that in spite of his wealth, he had nothing
"precious" with which to protect his own life.
Knowing that he was close to death and afraid to
die without first understanding how to cultivate
the Way, he went with his nephew to search for a
Good Knowing Advisor, one with the five eyes and

the six spiritual penetrations who could teach him
the fundamentals of dhyāna meditation. For three
years they wandered together, visiting famous Dharma Masters in well-known monasteries and great
scholars in the academies. They sought out hermits
in lonely mountain caves, but found no one who
could teach them dhyāna. Sad and disappointed,
they returned.

One day, the Master went down the mountain to
buy some oil, incense, and candles. On the way to
town, he stopped to rest at Kuan Chung Hsi's house.
When the nephew saw the Master, he was astonished.
Pulling his uncle aside he asked, "Who is that
monk? Last night I dreamed that he came here and
sat on the brick bed. I knelt before him and
begged him to teach us the Way. In the dream he
said, 'You have a pig skin on your body which must
come off before you can cultivate,' and he peeled
a layer of skin off my body and threw it on the
ground. It was a pig skin. 'You aren't a vegetarian,' the Master said, 'and you eat pork. In
the future you will have a pig skin on your back.'
I was scared stiff and said to him, 'Oh no! Pigs
are filthy and useless!' I had the dream last
night and now the monk is actually here. Is it a
lucky sign or not?"

His uncle was excited. "Really?" he said,
"did you really have that dream? Of course it's a
lucky sign. The monk is the Venerable Master Tu
Lun, Filial Son Pai. I've wished to bow to him
for a long time and now he's come here. It is true,
then, that he has the Way and he's brought it to
our house."

After talking they went into the room where
the Master was sitting, closed the door, and bowed.

"Have you both gone insane?" said the Master.
"What do you want from me? I'm just the same as
you. I don't understand the Way."

"We know you cultivate filial piety," said
the uncle, "and that you have come to show us the
Way. Last night my nephew dreamed you peeled a pig
skin off his body."

"You're confused," said the Master. "He's
not a pig. How could I peel a pig skin off him?
I can't teach you to cultivate, but if you want to
find a teacher, I can help you look."

"We've looked everywhere," they said, "but we
haven't found one. Wherever we go it's always the
same. They all have a lot of name and fame, but
no genuine virtue."

During the next two years the Master sent
them everywhere to meet all kinds of cultivators
and good knowing advisors. They continually insisted on taking the Master as their teacher, but
the Master was still a young novice and didn't
want any disciples. Finally, they knelt before
him and refused to get up. "It's useless to talk
about whether or not I have the Way," the Master
said. "First learn to sit in full lotus and then
I will teach you."

They practiced sitting every day. The nephew
had no trouble, but the uncle's bones were old and
and, in northeast China the mountain people have
big kneecaps which stick up about fifteen inches
in the air when they try to sit cross-legged. But
the uncle kept trying. He pushed his knees down
over and over, and in seventy days he finally ma-
naged to sit in full lotus. When the Master returned, he noticed that the uncle's legs were swol-
len. They were so sore, in fact, that he couldn't
even step over a cart rut. "You shouldn't sit in
full lotus," the Master told him. "Are you still
practicing?"

"I am," said the uncle.

"You shouldn't continue," said the Master.

"What do you mean?" said the uncle. "I'm a-
bout to die and if I don't practice now, what will
I do then? No matter what, I'm going to practice
meditation. If I die, that's another matter, but
as long as I'm still alive, I'm going to practice."

"Do what you like," said the Master, and he
left. When he returned a hundred days later he
noticed that the uncle's legs were no longer swol-
len. "You're not still sitting, are you?" he asked.

Kuan Chung Hsi smiled. "I can sit in full
lotus now," he said, "and no matter how long I sit,
it doesn't hurt, and my legs don't swell."

"Now," said the Master, "I'll teach you how
to work," and he instructed them saying:

"Why don't living beings attain the Way? It
is because of the false mind which disturbs the
true nature and binds them to their passions. Defiled by greed, frustration, and discursive thought,
they get caught in the flow of birth and death;
they sink into the sea of suffering and lose the
Way. But although the sea of suffering is boundless, a turn of the head is the other shore. Always be alert and watchful in meditation, like a
chicken watching its eggs, or a dragon guarding

its pearl. By and by you will get good news."
     The uncle was incredibly happy and sat in
meditation every day. When his death approached,
he gathered his family together and said, "On such
and such a day, at such and such a time, I'm going
to leave; I'm going to die. The only thing I still
desire is to see my teacher once again. But I
don't know where he is now, and so I cannot see
him." Then on the appointed day, he sat upright
in full lotus, and without an illness, died. That
evening, many of the villagers had the same dream;
they dreamed that they saw the uncle accompanied
by two youths in dark robes, being taken to the
West.
     Later, the nephew insisted on formally taking
the Master as his teacher. He followed the Master
down the road until they entered a clearing. Then
suddenly he knelt, clutched the Master's sleeve,
and begged to become a disciple. The Master brushed
him off and left, while the boy pleaded saying he
would not get up unless he was allowed to become a
disciple. The boy was truly filial and always respected his teacher, and although his family wasn't
rich, every New Year's he gave the Master a gift.
He was deeply sincere, and because of his dream
about the pig skin, he believed the Master to be
a living Bodhisattva.

     While the Master and Great Master Ch'ang Jen
were collecting offerings for the purpose of building temples, it was often the case that people
who had never seen the Master would have a dream
in which the Master clearly appeared. The following day, much to their astonishment, the Master
would invariably show up at their home on his
rounds. Recognizing the Master as the Bhiksu they
had seen in their dreams, they would be extremely
respectful towards him and deeply believe in him
and they were generous in their assistance in
raising funds. This was a common occurrence.

"THE BUDDHA HAS COME!"

     About thirty miles from Three Conditions Tem-
ple, in a little village called Hou Hsing Lung,
there lived one Ch'eng Shan Jen, "Good Man Ch'eng."
As a youth, he had set his great intelligence a-
side in order to smoke opium and gamble his ser-

vants' salaries away from them. At age forty, he
took refuge with the Old Abbot Ch'ang Jen.

After taking refuge, he changed his evil habits and cultivated merit and virtue so indust-
riously that he was soon known throughout the area
as "Good Man Ch'eng." Those without food could
always go to him for wheat and rice.

One year, one of his servants became possessed
by a demon. Insane, he tried to set fire to
Ch'eng's house and granaries, intent on destroying
his family and household. Finally, on New Year's
Eve, Good Man Ch'eng went to Three Conditions Temple and begged Abbot Ch'ang Jen for help; he truly
believed in the Old Abbot. The Abbot sent for the
Master.

"He asked you to help him," the Master said
to the Abbot. "Why give the trouble to me?"

"He's one of our good Dharma protectors," replied the Abbot. 'Won't you see what you can do?"

As the Old Abbot and the Master were like one
person, the Master agreed, and at Ch'eng's house
he sat on the high brick bed, facing the servant.
The servant threw his hands over his face. He himself had no idea he had been possessed.

"What are you doing?" said the Master.

"I can't see!" cried the servant. "I can't
see anything but light. Don't you see it?" The
servant stared and knelt before the Master.

"Why are you kneeling?" the Master asked.

"The Buddha has come," said the servant, and
in a moment he was better--the demon gone.

THE WISE YU

In Manchuria, the Master had a friend and
fellow cultivator who had been a thief. He had
changed his evil ways, however, and gone to practice filial piety beside his parents' graves.
While cultivating he opened a bit of wisdom, and
his teacher gave him the name "Wise Yu." What
made him change from a thief into a cultivator?

Once, while stealing, someone caught him and
shot him in the arm. Such a wound normally would
have healed in a month, but after a year, his still
hadn't. Because of that, he repented, "Ah!" he
said, "I was a thief and someone shot me. I'm
lucky even to be alive. But why is the wound taking so long to heal?" Then he made a vow, "If the

wound heals within a week, I will never steal a-
gain; I will go to sit beside my parents' graves
as an act of filial piety." Strangely enough, by
the end of the week his wound had completely healed,
and so he went off to cultivate filial piety.

The Master said, "Children practice filial
piety to show that they have not forgotten their
parents' kindness in raising them. What is the
use of a living person sitting beside a grave? It
has no use at all, unless you are able to do it.
If you can do it, it is very meaningful because it
is a difficult practice. Traditionally one sits
for three years. People forty or fifty years old,
whose minds are more settled, find it easier than
younger people, who find it extremely difficult.
There's no one to talk to, no one to help you out;
it's a great deal of suffering."

At that time, Filial Son Yu was only 21 years
old. His teacher, Tsung I, a Master of great virtue and spiritual power, taught him how to sit in
meditation, and Filial Son Yu worked hard. Then,
while he was sitting, a demon came--a fiery dragon.
It wound itself around him three times and scorched
him, hotter and fiercer every minute until his teacher finally defeated it and took it as a disciple.
After that the dragon became Filial Son Yu's Dharma Protector.

Once, after he had been practicing for two and
a half years, it rained for over a month and washed
out all the newly planted fields. Fearing that
people would starve, Filial Son Yu made another
vow, "If the sky clears within three days, I will
cut off a piece of my own flesh as an offering to
the Lord of Heaven." Because he had not yet studied the Buddhadharma, he wanted to make an offering to God.

In less than three days the sky cleared and
Filial Son cut off a piece of his flesh. The first
time he tried, it didn't come off, and so he cut
again, and then again, and finally succeeded in
cutting off about a pound of flesh. He fell to
the ground unconscious while the blood flowed over
an area of four feet, staining the soil bright red.

Before he passed out, a visitor ran to inform
the government, and the government sent an official to investigate and take part in the offering
to heaven. Many people were greatly influenced
by Filial Son Yu's act, and recognized him as a
great Bodhisattva.

     After that, people flocked to see him. A
bird also became his friend. The tiny bird could
talk, but all it would say was, "Do more virtuous
deeds. Do more virtuous deeds. The more virtuous
deeds you do, the better." Just like an old friend,
the bird would perch on his head, hands, and shoul-
ders and didn't fear him in the least. He helped
Filial Son Yu do his work and meditate, and sometimes the two of them cracked jokes and had a
great deal of fun. But when visitors came the
bird always flew off and would only return again
when they had left.
     When three weeks had passed and Filial Son
Yu's wound had healed, the bird left for good.
When his three years of filial piety had expired,
the Way Virtue Association invited him to join and
give lectures. He was a powerful speaker, and
taught countless people about the qualities of
virtue, humaneness, propriety, and so forth.
     At that time Chinese people didn't grow long
hair or beards, but as a filial son, Wise Yu had
let his hair and beard grow so that he looked much
like the present day hippies. He did not take
drugs, however; he ate pure vegetarian food, recited the Buddha's name, and spoke true principle.
Filial Sons let their hair and beards grow to accord with the line in the *Classic of Filial Piety* which
says, "Our body, skin, and hair came from our parents; not harming the body is in accord with the
Way." Not being destructive to your own body is
the beginning of filial piety.
     So you may wonder if he protected his long
hair and beard, why did he cut off a piece of his
own flesh? Is that filial? Wouldn't his parents
have cried had they seen him do such a thing?
     Filial Son Yu cut off his flesh seeking a re-
sponse from the Lord in Heaven for the benefit of
all. At that time he was unfamiliar with the *Classic of Filial Piety*. He had heard that people practiced filial conduct by sitting beside their parents' graves and so he also did it.
     Then, afraid that people might go hungry, he
simply decided to sacrifice his own flesh in order
to save them. With that one, true, sincere thought,
he sacrificed what others cannot sacrifice and so
obtained a response.
     While lecturing at the Way Virtue Association,
Filial Son Yu heard about the Master, who was also
cultivating filial piety and who was known as Filial

Son Pai. Filial Son Yu had been a bit arrogant
thinking, "I'm only 21 years old, and yet I'm cultivating filial piety." When he heard that the
Master was only 19 he felt he had been outdone and
decided he simply must meet the Master.

The Master also wished to meet Filial Son Yu,
and one day he happened to visit the Way Virtue
Association. He recognized Filial Son Yu at once
by his long hair and beard. The Master himself
had shaved his head. "You must be Good Man Yu,"
said the Master.

"And who are you?" said Filial Son Yu.

"You don't know me," the Master replied, "but
I know you. In fact, I don't know who I am. You
probably know who you are, but I don't know who I
am."

Filial Son Yu was startled. "Really?" he exclaimed. Then someone introduced them and Filial
Son Yu said, "Where did you come from?"

"I come from where I came," said the Master.

Filial Son Yu found his answer truly strange.
Then the Master asked, "And where are you going?"

"I'm not going anywhere," said the Filial Son.

"Then why did you ask me where I came from?"
said the Master, and the Filial Son grabbed his
hand, delighted.

The account of their meeting was told everywhere. The Master has said, "There's no place to
come from and no place to go. Neither coming nor
going and yet coming and going; one comes from
where one comes and goes to where one goes. One
of the Buddha's ten titles is 'The Thus Come One.'
The *Diamond Sūtra* says, 'Because he comes from nowhere and goes nowhere he is called the Thus Come
One.'"

When they first saw each other, neither the
Filial Son Yu nor the Filial Son Pai spoke. But
then Filial Son Yu became curious, and asked the
Master where he had come from. "The moment he
asked," the Master relates, "he knew he had made
a mistake. Why?

> *Open your mouth and you're wrong:*
> *Think up a thought and you're mistaken.*
> *Anything that can be spoken*
> *Is not the actual principle.*

That which can be spoken is not the ultimate
Dharma. The ultimate Dharma is neither spoken nor
transmitted. It should be viewed like that."

THE RESURRECTION

When asked by the Venerable Master Hsin Jen to assist in building a temple, the Master went to the village of Hsi Ta Chu to borrow wagons in order to haul materials to the building site, but no one was willing to help. When he spoke with the Mayor, Liu Chung Ch'in, the Mayor replied, "I am sorry, but right now we are extremely busy planting fields and need every available wagon."

That morning, the Mayor's sister-in-law's child died. She brought the child to the Master and asked, "Why did my child die? He was good and obedient."

"Have you been filial to your parents-in-law?" asked the Master. "No doubt you haven't and so your child has died. If you would like him back, bow to them and admit your errors. Then I will make your child live again."

Seeing her hesitate, the Master added, "I'm not kidding! Why would I joke about something like that? Go try it out!"

She went to her husband's family and bowed. "It's true," she said, "I haven't been filial and so my child has died." Soon the entire family was crying and apologizing. When she returned home she ran to her child but found him still dead.

"Is he better?" asked the Master.

"No," she said.

"Give him to me," said the Master. He took the child in his arms, patted it firmly on the head three times and the child began to cry. He was completely well. The entire household took refuge with the Master, and then the whole village took refuge, too. When the Mayor got word, he said, " "You asked to use our carts? You may take them all. We will all help you build the temple.

After that, wherever he went people fought to lend the Master a cart. Then the trouble came: "My mother is sick," said one. "Couldn't you help her?" Another said, "My uncle is not well..." In all cases, the Master exhausted his strength to cure the sick. "You have worked for the Buddhas and Bodhisattvas," he would say, "and they will certainly take care of you. From today on your sickness will be healed." In each case as soon as he spoke they were cured. Within a month, over eight hundred carts were available for his use.

It was winter and the Master rose at three in the morning and went to work in the snow, wear-

ing only three layers of cotton clothing. When
people saw him, they would exclaim, "He only eats
one meal a day and he's still not afraid of the
cold. Incredible!"

***

When Li Ch'ing Shan heard of the miraculous
recovery of the Liu child, he respectfully asked
the Master to cure his little brother. When the
Master entered the house, he said, "The house is
too full of darkness. There is nothing I can do.
Within a few days a great misfortune will occur."

Towards the end of the week, Li Ch'ing Shan
quarreled with his brother and committed suicide.
His brother and daughter died shortly thereafter.
The villagers said that the Master had knowledge
of the future, but the Master made no reply.

THE METHOD

The Master accompanied the Great Master Ch'ang
Jen encouraging people to make offerings of charity.
The two of them went everywhere. Once they passed
through a country village, and just as they were
about to enter the house of a Mr. Wong, he grabbed
his child and knelt before them in the doorway,
begging them to save his child's life. His child
had tuberculosis and coughed up blood and his stomach and head ached. Hearing his request, Great
Master Ch'ang Jen said, "Ask Dharma Master An Tz'u.
He can help you."

The Master replied, "The man asked you to help
him. Why do you give your work to me?" The Abbot
insisted, however, and so the Master agreed. Then
he asked Mr. Wong a strange question: "Do you want
your son to live? I am unable to save him. You
must save him yourself."

"I want him to live," said Mr. Wong. "But how
can I save him? I don't know how."

"Here is the method," said the Master. "If
you want him to live, you must allow him to leave
the home-life and become a Bhikṣu. If he leaves
home, he will live; if he does not, he will surely
die. There are no two ways about it."

The child was eleven years old at the time.
Mr. Wong's wife agreed to the conditions, and the
Master repeated them. "If your child leaves home,

from this very day he will not cough blood and his
stomach and head will be cured," he said.
"How do you feel?" they asked the boy.
"Better," he said. "In fact, I feel fine."
The child was soon completely well. Although
the Master advised Mr. Wong on several occasions to
bring his son to the temple, Mr. Wong did not do
so. The Master waited two or three months. One
day, as he was walking along the outskirts of the
village, the child, sitting at home, was aware of
his proximity. "Father," he said, "my teacher came
to our village today, but he did not stop at our
house. He is probably unhappy with us."
From that day, the child relapsed and his
sickness was worse than before. A week later his
father went to the temple, but the Master wasn't
there, and since none of the other people understood
the situation, no one could help him.
Arriving home, his son said, "I went with you
to the Temple today and saw every room and know
who lives where. One room was hung with banners
for the dead..."
"Strange," said his father. "Your mother says
you were here all the time. How could you have
gone with me to the Temple?"
A few days later the Master was again walking
on the outskirts of town, returning to the Temple,
and the child knew. "My teacher is returning to
the Temple; he's not stopping here. Please follow
his instructions and let me leave home right away.
Go and see him immediately."
"Wait until tomorrow," said his father. "I'll
go then."
"You don't have to go," said the boy. "Even
if you went this minute, it wouldn't make any difference."
That evening, at dusk, the child sat up in
bed. "Father?" he called. "Light the lamp and
tell me if I am sitting correctly."
His father lit the lamp and looked at his son
who was sitting serene and upright in full lotus.
He was dead.
No matter how hard his father and mother cried,
the child didn't come back to life. They begged
the Master to make him live again, but the Master
said, "The method was yours, not mine. I gave it
to you, but you didn't use it. There is nothing
more I can do."
Why did the Master instruct the child to
leave home? It was because he had the appearance

of a Bhikṣu, and in past lives he had made vows to leave home in every life.

AN OUTSTANDING EXAMPLE

In Shuang Ch'eng District, San Hsing Village, lived a man named Yen Yu K'un whose third son Shao Ying was a colonel in the army. When Shao Ying's regiment was stationed in San Chiang Province in 1942, he took his mother and sister there to live with him. His sister, Shu Lan, had not yet married, and soon Shao Ying arranged her betrothal to Colonel Pai. On the day before the wedding, Shu Lan suddenly fell ill and for several days lay unconscious in bed.

One day she suddenly said to her mother, "The White-robed Kuan Yin is coming. Quick, light incense as an offering!" and then she rose and prostrated herself before the altar. Her moving lips showed that she was speaking with someone, and at length she gestured as if saying a respectful farewell to an honored guest. Then she turned to her mother, saying, "Kuan Yin has just told me that my illness will be cured if I do not marry but leave the home-life and cultivate the Way. She has agreed that I may leave the home-life after the death of my parents. Tommorrow a Dharma Master will come to heal me."

Her mother was pleased, and the following day the gong before Shu Lan's altar spontaneously sounded three times. Just then a Dharma Master entered the room, wearing a monk's cap and rag robe. He was barefoot and carried the white whisk brush which is used to dispell illness. He appeared in this manner three times daily for nine days. Finally, he said, "Shu Lan, can you leave the home-life without any doubts?"

"When I am well," she said, "I shall most certainly leave home to cultivate." The Master then handed her a pill. She swallowed it and recovered immediately.

While Shu Lan was dangerously ill, her mother had wired her father. When he arrived, she was well, and he scoffed when he heard the events surrounding her recovery. "No doubt they were just hallucinations brought on by a high fever. They are nothing but the products of her delirium, for how else could an ordinary human being see a Bodhisattva?"

Hearing his words, Shu Lan herself doubted her experiences and returned to San Hsing Village with her father and mother. Later she had a dream in which Maitreya Bodhisattva said, "Your father will die within seven days. Recite the Buddha's name to lessen his offenses."

When she told her father the next morning, he did not believe her. Against his daughter's protests, on the sixth day after the dream, he set out for Shuang Ch'eng where he bought some things. He went to the railway station to buy his return ticket and just as he entered the gate he suddenly fainted. The police informed the Yang family and by the time Shu Lan's father was carried home, he was dead. That happened exactly seven days after her dream.

Shu Lan's other brother Shih Ch'ao not only obstructed his sister's attempts to leave home, but slandered the Buddha, Dharma, and Saṅgha as well. One night he dreamed that a Bodhisattva spoke to him saying, "In a month you will die!" He awoke, surprised, but did not repent and died within a month, on the 13th day of the 5th month, 1945.

That year, on the 25th day of the 12th month, the Master paid a special visit to Shu Lan's house. The moment she saw the Master, Shu Lan exclaimed, "Mother! The Dharma Master who cured my illness in San Chiang Province has now come here." She rose to greet him and bowed reverently.

The Master said, "So you still recognize me?"

"Yes," said the girl.

"Do you still wish to leave the home-life?" he asked.

"Before, in my confusion, I didn't understand. I had no proof and so I doubted," she replied. "Now I know it is true. The Master has manifested as a Bodhisattva to cure my illness. I am determined to leave home. How could there be any question?"

From that time on, Shu Lan ate a strict vegetarian diet and constantly recited the Buddha's name. She set an outstanding example among her peers and convinced her three brothers and many of her relatives, the young and the well-educated, of the truth of Buddhism. They all took refuge with the Triple Jewel and bowed to the Master as their teacher.

A WHITE FOX SEEKS REFUGE

In Shuang Ch'eng District, in the Fourth District of Hsiang Pai Ch'i, was a family named Hsia which supported a fox immortal named Hu T'ien Pai and his retinue of over 300. The immortal dispensed medicines and used all manner of spiritual powers to save people, sometimes transforming himself into an old man in order to give the townspeople good advice and exhort them to practice virtue. Thus, he was admired by the community. One day he addressed his assembly as follows:

"In three years I shall take refuge with the Buddhist Triple Jewel and follow my compassionate teacher to cultivate the Way."

When three years had passed, the Master arrived as prophesied, and the immortal and his retinue took refuge with the proper teaching. They cultivated merit and virtue with great vigor and upheld the Dharma, teaching many living beings how to leave suffering and attain bliss.

A HEAVENLY DEMON TAKES REFUGE WITH THE TRIPLE JEWEL

On the twelfth day of the second month in the year of 1945, the Master passed through the Chou family station in Northeast China. In the town there was a Way Virtue Association which met daily for lectures on the Way and its Virtue. Because many of the members were the Master's disciples, whenever he traveled near that town, he stayed for a few days.

This time the Master met a Chinese astrologer named Chou who cast his horoscope. The astrologer said, "You should be an official. Why have you left home? Had you wanted to, you could have been a great official."

"I haven't any idea how to be an official," the Master said, "but I do know how to be a Buddhist Bhikṣu, and so I have left home."

"What a pity," said the astrologer, and he looked at the Master's hand. "At the very least," he said, "you could have been a top-ranking Imperial scholar."

"No," said the Master, "I couldn't even have come in last."

"Oh," the astrologer added, "this year some-

thing very lucky will happen to change your life.
After the tenth or twelfth of next month things
will be different. Right now, all the people within 350 miles believe in you, but after the tenth
of next month, everyone within 3500 miles will believe in you."
     "How is that?" asked the Master.
     "When the time comes, you will know," he said.
     Two days later, the Master went to the village
of Hsiang Pai Ch'i, fourth district, and stayed
with his disciple Hsia Tsun Hsiang, who was over
60 years old. Mr. Hsia was the richest landowner
in the area and had never believed in Buddhism until he saw the Master and immediately decided to
take refuge with him. He and his family of over
thirty people all took refuge and every time the
Master visited them, they were extremely happy. On
this occasion the Master stayed for ten days and
in that time 72 people took refuge.
     On the twenty-fifth, the Master set out in Mr.
Hsia's cart for the city of Shuang Ch'eng. Although
it was early spring, the weather was bitter cold.
The driver and the attendant were dressed in fur
coats, trousers, and hats, but the Master wore only
his usual rag robe made of three layers of thin
cotton cloth, trousers made of two layers of cloth,
open Arhat sandals with no socks, and a pointed
hat that didn't cover his ears.
     They rode from three in the morning until dawn,
arriving in Shuang Ch'eng at seven in the morning.
The attendant and the driver had stopped repeatedly
to exercise and keep warm, but the Master had re-
mained in the cart. When they arrived and the
Master got out of the cart, the driver exclaimed,
"We thought surely you had frozen to death!"
     The Master stayed with friends, Dharma pro-
tecting laymen, for a few days, and on the ninth
day of the third month, he returned to Hsia Tsun
Hsiang's home in Hsiang Pai Ch'i. Upon arriving,
he was told that one of his recent disciples, the
daugher of Hsia Wen Shan, had fallen dangerously
ill. She hadn't eaten, slept, or drunk water for
over a week. She did not speak, and she looked
fiercely angry as if she wanted to beat people.
     Then her mother came. "Master," she said,
"my daughter became very ill not less than a week
after taking refuge," and she described her illness.
     The Master said, "I can't cure her, but my
disciple Han Kang Chi has opened his five eyes and

knows people's past, present, and future affairs.
You should ask him."

Han Kang Chi had also taken refuge in Shuang
Ch'eng on the twenty-fourth of the second month.
At first, the Master had refused to take him as a
disciple because before the Master had left home,
the two of them had been good friends and had
worked together in the Way Virtue Association. After the Master left home and Han Kang Chi opened
his five eyes, he looked at the Master and saw
that, life after life, the Master had always been
his teacher.

"But if I don't take refuge with you I know
that in this life I shall certainly fall," Han Kang
Chi said, and he knelt on the ground determined to
take refuge.

The Master was just as determined not to accept him, but Han knelt for perhaps a half an hour
when the Master finally said, "Those who take refuge with me must offer up their conduct in accord
with the teaching. You have talent; you know the
past, present, and future. Is it possible that it
has caused you to become arrogant? Will your pride
prevent you from obeying instructions?"

"Master," he said, "I will certainly obey. If
you tell me to throw myself into a cauldron of
boiling soup, I'll do it; if you tell me to walk
on fire, I'll walk. I'll stand at my post and not
resign. If I get boiled or burned to death, that's
all right."

"You'd better be telling the truth," said the
Master. "If I give you instructions, you can't ignore them."

"No matter what it is," he said, "If you tell
me to do it, I will do it, and fear no danger whatever."

And so Han Kang Chi was one of the seventy-
two who took refuge on the twenty-fourth.

When the Master heard that one of his disciples was sick, he told Hang Kang Chi, "You can
diagnose illnesses. Take a look."

Han Kang Chi sat in meditation and made a con-
templative examination of the illness. Suddenly
his face blanched with terror. "Master," he said,
"we can't handle this one. It's beyond our control. The demon who is causing the illness is extremely violent and can assume human form to bring
chaos into the world and injury to humankind."

"What makes the demon so fierce?" asked the
Master.

"The demon was a ghost long ago in the Chou
dynasty,"1 he said. "Because it didn't behave
properly, a man with spiritual powers shattered it
with thunder.2 But the ghost's spirit did not completely disperse and it later fused into a powerful demon which could fly--and vanish--and appear,
at will.

"The demon has refined some dharma treasures,"
he continued. "The first is an exclusive anti-
thunder device: a black hat made out of human af-
terbirth. Thunder has a great aversion to filth.
She also has two round balls. When she hits someone with one of them, he immediately dies. If she
puts her hat on someone, his mind falls under her
control, and he becomes one of her retinue. Master, we can't manage such a fierce demon."

"Then what will become of the sick girl?" the
Master asked.

"She will certainly die," he said.

"If she weren't my disciple I'd pay no attention, but she took refuge with me, so I can't allow the demon to take her life."

"You take care of it, then," said Han Kang
Chi, "but I'm not going."

"What?" said the Master. "You said you would
jump into the soup, walk on fire, and stay at your
post without resigning. It's not even soup or
fire. Why have you suddenly decided to resign?"

Han Kang Chi thought it over. "If you appoint
some Dharma Protectors to take care of me..." he
said.

"Don't shilly-shally!" said the Master. "If
you're going to go, go, but don't wobble!"

When they arrived, they saw the girl lying on
the bed with her head and knees on the bed and the
rest of her body sticking up in the air at an ab-
surd angle. Her eyes were as wide as those of an
ox, and she glared with rage at the Master.

1122-255 B.C.

2Westerners think that thunder has no one control-
ling it, and while that may be the case for ordinary thunder, there is a special kind of thunder
which is used by gods to subdue and conquer the
strange demons and ghosts who wander throughout
the world.

The Master asked the girl's family, "What is
the cause of the illness?"

"A few days ago," they said, "a strange old
woman was seen sitting beside a deserted grave,
crying mournfully, 'Oh, my person, oh my person...'
She was wearing a dark blue gown and had braided
her hair backwards in two plaits which went up her
head in back and hung down across her temples.
She was wearing yellow trousers and shoes and carried a black hat. Hearing her cries, old Mrs.
Hsia went to comfort her, but she continued to
cry, 'Oh my person, oh my person.'

"The two of them walked to the village gate,
but the old woman wouldn't go in. The village was
surrounded by a wall and had a gate on each of the
four sides. The old woman stood outside the gate,
crying. Just then Hsia Tsun Hsiang's horsecart
came over the hill toward the village. When it
reached the gate the horse saw the woman and reared
in fright, for horses can recognize things people
cannot see. As the horsecart went careening through
the gate, the old woman followed it in. Probably
the spirit who guards the gate had his back turned,
and in the confusion, she went sneaking through.

"The old woman ran to the house of Mr. Yu
Chung Pao and continued to cry for her 'person.'
Then she ran out of the house and up the street,
followed by thirty or forty curious onlookers who
jeered at her. 'Stupid old woman!' they said,
'what's your last name?'

"'I don't know,' she said.

"'What's your first name?' they said.

"'I don't know. I'm a corpse and don't know
anything about the affairs of the world.'

"She continued to walk as if in a stupor until she reached the back wall of Hsia Wen Shan's
estate. She then threw her hat over the eight foot
wall, and in one jump, lept right over after it.

"'The old woman can do magical gymnastics!'
the crowd screeched, and they ran around to the
front gate and peeped in.

"Hsia Wen Shan, another who had taken refuge
on the twenty-fourth, ran in the door. 'Mama!
Mama!' he cried, 'the old woman is in our house,
but don't be afraid.'

"His mother looked out the window, but saw
nothing strange. When she turned around, there
was the old woman crawling up on the k'ang. She
was half way on the k'ang and half way on the floor.

"'What do you want?' shouted the mother, but the old woman made no reply..."

Now, when the seventy-two people took refuge, the Master taught them all to recite the Great Compassion Mantra and advised them to use it in times of danger and distress, so that Kuan Yin Bodhisattva would protect them, and a lot of people had been reciting the Great Compassion Mantra in that village. Seeing the old woman's strange appearance, the mother and her daughter began immediately to recite the mantra. Just as they recited the first line "Na mwo he la da nwo do la ye ye," the old woman slunk to the ground and lay inert, exactly like a corpse.

Seeing that, the family was greatly upset. "If someone dies in our house, the police are sure to investigate," they said.

They went for the sheriff who picked the old woman up with one hand, and set her outside. Then he took her to the courthouse for questioning. "Where are you from?" he asked, "and why have you come here?"

"Don't ask me," she said. "I'm a corpse. I have no name and no home. I just live wherever I am."

Frightened, the sheriff escorted her at pistol point some fifty paces outside the village, but when he returned to the village gate, she was right behind him. He took her seventy paces and she followed him back again. Finally, he and three deputies took her 150 paces outside the city and said, "Get out or get shot!" and they fired two shots in the air.

The old woman fell to the ground in terror, thinking the shots were thunder which had destroyed her before, and she didn't follow them back to the village.

When the sheriff and his men returned they heard that Hsia Wen Shan's daughter was sick, not speaking, eating, or sleeping, but just lying on the bed staring in rage with her head on the pillow and her bottom sticking straight up in the air.

The Master said to Han Kang Chi, "You said that if we tried to handle the matter we would die. Well, I would rather die than not save one of my disciples. First of all, I must save those who have taken refuge with me; I can't stand by and let them die. Secondly, I must save the demon. You say no one can control her, but she has com-

mitted so many offenses there's bound to be someone
who can subdue her. If she were to be destroyed,
it would be a great pity for she has cultivated
diligently for many years. Even if she has enough
talent to kill me, I'll still save her. Finally,
I must save all living beings in the world, and if
I don't subdue her now, in the future many people
will be harmed by her. For these three reasons,
then, I'm going to work."

Just then the sheriff happened by and overheard the discussion in which the old woman was
referred to as a demon. "No wonder!" he exclaimed.
"That's why I was able to pick her up with one
hand, just as if there were nothing there at all.
It didn't occur to me at the time, but now I realize she's a demon."

The Master employed one of the Five Kinds of
Dharmas[1] in the Sūraṅgama Mantra, that of "summoning and hooking," to catch the demon. When the
demon woman entered the room, she had about her
an intense and nauseating stench. She tried to
put her dharma treasure, the black hat, on the
Master's head, but couldn't get it on him. She
tried to hit him with one of her magic balls, but
it didn't work. She threw the second ball and
missed again. Knowing she was finished, she turned
to run, but when she first arrived the Master had
laid a net which would trap her no matter where
she tried to go. Now the Master called in the
gods, dragons, and others of the eight-fold division of ghosts and spirits, as well as Dharma Protectors and good spirits, who watched from the
left, right, front, rear, downwards, upwards, and
in the intermediate directions. Seeing that she
couldn't get away, she knelt and wept.

The Master spoke the Dharma for her, explaining the Four Holy Truths, the Twelve Links, and
the Six Perfections, and she immediately understood, resolved to realize Bodhi, and asked to
take refuge with the Triple Jewel. The Master ac-
cepted her and gave her the name, "Vajra As-You-
Will Maiden."

---

[1]They are: 1) stopping calamities, 2) creating aus-
piciousness, 3) summoning and hooking (calling
strange creatures and demons), 4) subduing and con-
quering, and 5) calling in the aid of the Buddhas
and Bodhisattvas.

     She followed the Master when he went to save
people, but her basic make-up was that of a demon,
and no matter where she went she carried her over-
whelming stench. The Master sent her to Chiao Ho
County in Chi Lin Province to Lui Fa Mountain to
cultivate the Way in the Transparent Cave of the
Ten Thousand Saints.[1] She cultivated vigorously

---

[1]The cave is called "Ten Thousand Saints." The Master has sent many of his strange, unusual disciples
there to cultivate. It is said to be transparent
because it has three entrances and is totally vi-
sible from all directions. Where the three tun-
nels meet there is a temple made of bricks and lum-
ber which were carried up the steep mountain crags
on the backs of goats. Off the western entrance
there is a cave called "The Cave of Lao Tzu." Off
the eastern entrance is "The Dripping Water Cave,"
which drips enough water to satisfy the thirst of
a hundred thousand horses. The cave in the back
is called "Chi Tsu Cave," named after Chi Hsiao
T'ang, a native of Northeast China who, in the Ming
dynasty, employed five ghosts, one of whom was the
"Black Fish Essence." The "Black Fish Essence" was
a Ming dynasty official in Peking called "Blackie
the Great." Chi Hsiao T'ang knew he was really a
fish and was determined to capture him. He knew
that "Blackie" would pass by the mountain and so
he waited for him. When he passed by, Chi Hsiao
T'ang released thunder from the palm of his hand
and killed him.
     No one actually knows how many caves there
are in Lui Fa Mountain. Each time you count them,
the number is different--today seventy-two, the
day following maybe seventy.
     A man once went there and watched two old men
playing chess in a cave when at last he coughed and
the two long-bearded men said to themselves, "How
did he get here?" and waved their hands in front
of the entrance which then closed by itself. The
man knelt right there seeking the Way from them until he finally died. His grave may still be seen
outside the Stone-Door Cave. How sincerely the
ancients sought the Way!
     Many worthy saints are there. One is Li Ming
who has mastered *kung fu* and can run up the steep
mountainside as fast as a monkey. When the Master
visits the cave he arrives at four in the morning
and often sees Li Ming Fu there bowing to the

and soon attained spiritual powers and could rescue living beings. But when she rescues them she
doesn't like it to be known, since good done for
others to see is not true good, and evil done in
secret in fear that others will know, is truly
great evil.

Thus, the former demon woman, having changed
her deviant ways and returned to orthodox practices, is now just the same as Kuan Yin Bodhisattva, having joined the Buddha's family.

The Power of Great Compassion over Death

Li Sheng Hsi of Harbin quarreled with his wife
over some trifle and she tried to kill herself by
drinking two cups of lye. By the time she was
discovered, it seemed impossible to save her.
Luckily, a Buddhist layman was present. "Dharma
Master Tu Lun is in the area," he said, "staying
with Mr. Kuo. Go quickly and implore his aid. He
can certainly work a miracle."

Mr. Li sent his son to the Master to beg for
help, but the Master said, "I work no miracles.
You had best call a doctor immediately."

When the boy reported the Master's words, the
layman said, "You must try again, and be even more
sincere. Unless one is truly sincere, the Master
won't meddle in other people's business."

The second time the boy knelt for three quar-
ters of an hour, crying bitterly. Convinced he
was in earnest, the Master returned with him and
took a look at the woman. Her four limbs were as
cold as ice and the family was already arranging
her funeral. Seeing the Master, the entire household bowed before him with their heads on the floor
and cried, "The Buddha has come to our aid!" The
Master bade them not to be afraid and said he would

Buddha, his hair matted in a lump which weighs
seven or eight pounds and which he never washes.
His facial features--eyes, ears, mouth, and nos-
trils--and his body, are very small, but he is
strong and alone can carry two railroad tracks so
heavy that eight ordinary men would be necded to
carry one. No one knows how old he is or where he
is from. These are not ancient fairy tales, they
are true events. If you believe them, they're
true; if you don't, they are still true.

help them. Then he blessed a glass of water with
the Great Compassion Mantra, pried the woman's
mouth open with a chopstick and poured the water
in her mouth. After a moment, some liquid bubbled
from the corners of her mouth, she vomited, and
was soon completely well. The Master then exhorted
the family to cooperate and live in harmony.

To express their deep gratitude, the family
has inscribed a plaque with the words, "As Master-
ful as the Tathāgata" written horizontally, and a
two line couplet on either side which reads, "Compassion saves all. The faithful are delivered to
realize the right enlightenment/Disasters are a-
verted. The spirit is revived to enlighten to the
unproduced."

GREAT COMPASSION CURES ILLNESS

In the autumn of 1945, a severe epidemic
spread across the countryside, killing scores of
people daily. In the Lu family village of Yu Fang
lived a family of eleven people named Mei. When
the plague struck their house, thirteen of them
were dead within three days, the two extra being
a son-in-law and a servant.

The Master asked several of his close disciples, "Do you want to go help people?"

"Yes," they said.

"All right," said the Master, "let's get to
work."

They walked to the village which had been ra-
vaged by the plague and began to circumambulate
the entire area while reciting the Great Compassion Mantra. The recitation cleansed the area and
everywhere they passed, the sickness was dispelled
and no further cases were reported. In this way
he saved countless living beings from disaster.

EVERY WISH IS FULFILLED

P'an Chi Shih of Shuang Ch'eng County was the
wealthiest man in the village. At forty years of
age, however, he and his wife were still childless
and longed for a son to continue the family line.
Hearing of the Master's awesome virtue, the couple
sought him out and immediately bowed to him as
their teacher. Under his guidance, they studied

the teachings, practiced dhyāna meditation, and
prayed to Kuan Yin Bodhisattva to fulfill their
wish. When the Master suggested that they offer
half of their wealth to benefit living beings,
they followed his instructions, rebuilding temples,
installing Buddha images, and supporting the Triple Jewel in all of its activities. At the end
of a year a son was born to them. They named him
Shih Te, "virtuous giving," and he was exception-
ally intelligent and wise. From then on, Mr. P'an
cultivated even more diligently, reading Sūtras,
reciting the Buddha's name, and doing good deeds
with all his might.

THE PRECIOUS SEAL

In Ta Nan Kou, in the city of Harbin, there
lived a young boy named Kao Te Fu, who was by nature very filial. His mother was an opium addict,
and her addiction had left her immobile, incapable
of even smoking opium, Her lips were split and
bleeding and her tongue had turned black. Chinese
and Western doctors both said she would surely
die, but her son said, "No! She cannot die. I
will cut off my hand as a sincere offering to the
Buddhas and Bodhisattvas. I am sure they will
come to my aid."
He went to Three Conditions Temple to make an
offering in order to save his mother's life. The
boy knelt down, unwrapped the butcher knife which
he had brought wrapped in a newspaper, and raised
it high in the air, when suddenly someone grabbed
him from behind. "Stop!" he said. "You can't
commit suicide here!"
"I am doing this to save my mother's life,"
replied the boy. "You can't stop me!"
Just then, the Abbot Ch'ang Jen's closest lay
disciple, Li Ching Hua, happened by and took the
boy to meet the Old Abbot. The Abbot sent for the
Master and asked for his help.
"But I'm just a novice," the Master said,
"Why do you insist on giving your work to me?"
"Be compassionate," said the Abbot.
The Master said to the boy, "Ride your by-
cycle home and I will follow shortly."
"Do you know the way?" said the boy.
"Never mind about me," said the Master, "just
go home."

The boy left as the sun was setting; it was about 5:00 in the afternoon. The boy took the main road and the Master took a smaller road. When the boy arrived home he was surprised to see the Master sitting there waiting for him. "Old cultivator," he said, "how did you get here before me?"

"Perhaps you stopped to play ball or watch a movie," said the Master. "In any case, your bicycle isn't as fast as mine and so I got here first."

When the Master saw the boy's mother, he was convinced that there was nothing he could do, but he decided to try anyway. He wrote out a Precious Seal which read:

> *"This boy is so sincere that he tried to cut off his hand to save his mother's life. Now that I have prevented him from doing this, no matter what, this woman must not die."*

"If she dies, King Yama," he said, "I'll be impolite to you." The Master sealed it and sent it off. He employed a dharma to extend her life, and finally, at three in the morning, he went to rest. The woman had been in a coma for seven days but the next morning she sat up. "Chu Tzu, Chu Tzu," she said, calling her son by his nickname, "I'm hungry. Bring me some rice gruel."

The boy ran to his mother, overjoyed; he had not heard her call his name for seven days. "Ma ma," he cried. "You were sick for so many days! Are you well now?"

"I was in a cave without the light of the sun, moon, or stars, or a lamp," she said. "I ran for many days, looking for my home. I called out, but got no response. Then I met a monk in rag robes who guided me back home."

"What did the monk look like?" asked her son.

"He was very tall," she said.

"Is that him?" said the boy pointing at the Master.

"Yes!" she exclaimed. "He's the one who brought me back!"

The entire family--sons and daughters, young and old--came to bow before the Master, and then the whole village took refuge with him saying, "Whatever you tell us to do, we will gladly follow your instructions."

PART VI: DISCIPLES

Kuo Neng, layname Lu, was the first disciple
to leave home under the Master. He was a tailor.
Although he made lots of money, his girlfriend
smoked opium, and no matter how much money he gave
her, it was never enough. When he realized how
wicked she was, he decided to leave home. When he
appeared, penniless and tattered, at Master Ju
Kuang's temple, Master Ju Kuang said, "You're too
poor. Go away."

Kuo Neng sat in the temple courtyard until
the gates were closed and he was bounced. He returned to his hotel where the opening of a new
vegetarian restaurant was taking place. The manager called to him, "My master is here. Come and
meet him." When they met, Kuo Neng was shy and
embarrassed, hardly daring to look at the Master.

"Why are you so upset?" the Master asked.

"I haven't any money..." said Kuo Neng. "But
why have you come here?"

The Master smiled. "I've come to get you,"
he said.

"What for?" asked Kuo Neng.

"To leave home, of course," said the Master.

Kuo Neng was startled. He hadn't told anyone
he wanted to leave home. "Let's go," said the
Master, "before your girlfriend gets back."

"But I don't have a robe!" said Kuo Neng.

"Here," said the Master, and he took off his
outer robe and gave it to Kuo Neng. The two of
them set out in the winter snow for Three Conditions Temple.

At the temple, Kuo Neng did bitter work; he
did the things no one else wanted to do: cooking,

cleaning, and carrying water. One day he built
himself a fine brick bed. "Who gave you permission to build this?" said the Master when he saw
it.

Kuo Neng stared at his shoes. "No one," he
said.

"Do you think you can do whatever you please?
You're not the manager here, are you?" said the
Master.

"No," said Kuo Neng. "What shall I do now?"

"Tear it down!" said the Master. "Then light
a stick of 'gold nail incense' and kneel before
the Buddha until it burns down." (About three hours.)

Later, when the Master went into the main
hall, he saw that Kuo Neng wasn't kneeling, he was
mending clothes.

"Why aren't you kneeling?" the Master asked.

"Did you really mean it?" said Kuo Neng.

"I am truly ashamed," said the Master. "It's
my fault that you aren't kneeling. If I had any
virtue at all my disciples would listen to my instructions. Since it's my fault, I'll just have
to kneel myself," and he knelt down.

"Oh no!" said Kuo Neng, and he ran to the
Master. "Don't do that! It's my fault, I'll
kneel!" But the Master paid no attention to him.
After that, he and the other disciples always listened to what the Master said.

THE SOGGY BISCUIT

While in Manchuria, the Master had a fourteen
year old attendant who wanted to obtain spiritual
powers. The Master told him it would not be difficult as long as he did not fear suffering. The
boy believed him and followed him for a year, enduring the unendurable, eating the inedible, and
doing what others cannot do.

One day, when invited to a layman's house to
receive offerings, the Master and child sat in meditation, as was their custom, for two hours before retiring. After an hour, however, the child
lay down to sleep. The Master grabbed his pillow
and threw it roughly on the floor. The child never slacked off again, whether the Master was with
him or not.

Once, while traveling the roads after a heavy
rain, they were about half-way home when the boy

spied a piece of pastry in the mud. "Master," he
said, "look at that!"
     "Eat it," said the Master.
     The boy laughed the remark off, and when they
got home, the Master said, "It's a pity that you
didn't eat the biscuit, because if you had, you
would have obtained your spiritual powers."
     "Really?" said the boy. "I'll go eat it right
away!"
     "It's too late now," said the Master. The
boy began to cry, but the Master consoled him.
     "Don't worry," he said. "There will be many
more chances." And in fact, shortly after that
he opened his heavenly eye, gained the knowledge
of other's thoughts, and knew the causes and ef-
fects of the past, present, and future. He attained the Way quickly because he was young, pure,
and without false thoughts.
     The Master had six or seven such disciples in
Manchuria and they helped him a great deal, traveling with him everywhere to spread the Buddha's
Teaching and relieve suffering. They believed in
the Master implicitly and would do whatever he
told them to do. In fact, if he had told them to
jump into a pit of fire or into the ocean, they
would have jumped without hesitation. Of course,
the Master would never have told them to do such
a thing, but the point is that they would follow
his instructions to the letter.
     It is the Master's hope that there will be
such people in America. That is why he is stern
in his teachings and encourages his disciples to
undertake ascetic practices. An ancient has said,
"Having tasted the bitterness within bitterness,
one can become a man above men." The harder you
cultivate, the sooner you will attain the Way. The
sooner you attain the Way, the sooner you will be
able to help mankind.

KUO SHUN

     Yao Kuo Shun was a native of Ta Nan Kou Vil-
lage which is located about eighteen miles from
Three Conditions Temple. Although young in years,
he was known to the villagers as "Old Yao" and he
drank, gambled, shot morphine, and smoked opium.
Finally, fed up with these meaningless pursuits,
Old Yao decided to cultivate the Way and put an
end to suffering once and for all.

     In the autumn of 1944, he left his home in
search of a Good Knowing Advisor, but was unfortu
nately taken prisoner by the Japanese and put in a
work camp on the Amur River which forms the border
between Russia and Manchuria. He never got enough
to eat and he never had enough to wear. Cold and
hungry, he thought of nothing but escape, but how
was he to find a way over the high electric barbed-
wire fence?
     After two and a half months, he had a dream
which a white-bearded old man appeared and said,
"Don't attempt an escape yet. I'll let you know
when the time is right." Kuo Shun waited and fifteen days later, the old man appeared again. "Today you can escape," he said. "Follow the white
dog."
     Kuo Shun and his partner grabbed their straw
mats and ran. Once outside, they saw a small white
dog who led them along the fence. They ran until
the dog came to a sudden halt and jumped over the
fence. Kuo Shun threw his mat on the wire and
scrambled over. His partner's mat caught fire,
however, and he didn't make it out.
     Once over the fence, Kuo Shun ran until dawn,
and by the time he stopped running he had seen
through all the misery of the world of people.
his attachments, and made up his mind to become a
Bhiksu.
     Coincidentally, the day of his return to Ta
Nan Kou was the very day of the Master's arrival
there to cure Kao Te Fu's mother, the opium addict.
The word of her miraculous recovery spread throughout the village, and hearing of it, Kuo Shun went
directly to Three Conditions Temple, where he met
the Old Master Ch'ang Jen and begged to be allowed
to leave home. The Old Abbot, suspicious of his
ragged appearance, refused him.
     Kuo Shun left, but immediately returned with
an offering of five pounds of fruit, and went instead before the Master where he knelt most respectfully. The Master turned his back on him and said
nothing. About two hours later, the Master finally
turned around and Kuo Shun was still there, kneeling. "Why, I'd forgotten all about you," said the
Master. "What do you want?"
     "I want to leave home," said the boy.
     "Leave home?" said the Master. "Do you have
a home?"
     "No," said Kuo Shun, "I guess I don't."

"If you don't have a home, how can you leave home? Never mind," said the Master. "I'll accept you."

Kuo Shun was speechless with joy.

"However," the Master continued, "you should know that to cultivate the Way at home is not easy, and to cultivate it having left home is even more difficult. It is said that before one has understood the most important business of life, it is as if one had lost his father and mother; after having understood it, it is even more like that. You must be able to bear what others cannot bear, yield where others cannot yield, eat what others cannot eat, endure what others cannot endure, practice what others cannot practice, live where others cannot live, humble yourself to serve others and always be unselfish. Most importantly,

> *In every thought, do not forget*
> *   the pain of birth and death.*
> *With all your heart, seek to escape*
> *   the rim of the turning wheel.*
> *Smash to pieces empty space;*
> *   comprehend the Buddha nature.*
> *Understand, and then the cloud*
> *   of delusion will fall away*
> *   --you'll see the basic nature.*

"This is the Dharma-ending age," the Master continued, "and although many leave home,   few realize the Way. Since you have left home with a sincere heart, you should establish yourself with firm resolve, and great vows. Bring forth the heart of Bodhi and be a steady flame, shining brightly in the strongest wind, pure gold in the raging fire. In the future, when your work is accomplished, you will glorify the Teaching."

From that day on, Kuo Shun did bitter work. He washed walls, scrubbed floors, and never complained. He ate one meal a day and never lay down. Cultivating the Pure Land and dhyāna meditation, he recited the Buddha's name one hundred thousand times a day, and often entered dhyāna samādhi for twenty-four hour periods in which he clearly understood the workings of cause and effect in the past, present, and future. Later, it was well known that, although Kuo Shun's hut was nearly seven miles from the temple, whenever the Master needed him all he had to do was call in his thoughts and Kuo Shun would hear and respond.

THE DEDICATION OF DRAGON RAIN COTTAGE

In 1945, after months of hard work, Kuo Shun built a small hut in Ta Nan Kou Village near the Temple of the Dragon King. When it was completed, he invited the Master to dedicate it, and the Master arrived with his disciples Kuo Neng, Kuo Chih, Kuo Tso, and others to perform the ceremony. That evening, the ten local dragon gods came and bowed before the Master, saying that they wished to take refuge with the Triple Jewel.

"It hasn't rained here in a long time," the Master said. "You receive the offerings of the people as spirits of the rains. Why don't you cause the rain to fall? If it rains tomorrow, I'll take you as my disciples. Otherwise, I don't want you."

"But the Lord of Heaven hasn't given us orders to make it rain," they said. "We can't do something like that without his permission."

"Then tell him there's a cultivator here who doesn't ask for much," said the Master, "just rain within forty miles of where he is. Outside of forty miles, I don't care if it rains or not."

The next day a heavy rain soaked an area of exactly forty miles around the hut. The dragons became disciples and each received the same Dharma name. Their first name was "Quickly Cultivate" and their last name was "Hurry and Save," that is, quickly cultivate the Way and then hurry and save all your dragon friends. The Master told them to give all their friends the name "Quickly Cultivate, Hurry and Save" as well. It is not known how many dragons have this name now. Because of this incident, Kuo Shun's hut became known as "Dragon Rain Cottage."

After the dedication of Dragon Rain Cottage, two ardent Buddhist disciples, Mr. Liu and Mr. Yang An Tzu, stayed at the hut to cultivate with Kuo Shun. They performed morning and evening recitations and recited the Great Compassion Mantra continuously. Mr. Liu then left the home-life and Mr. Yang was called into the army.

During his first two years of service, Mr. Yang often wrote to his family, but in the autumn of 1948, all correspondence suddenly ceased. One evening, six or seven months later, Kuo Shun was chanting the Great Compassion Mantra with Mr. Kao

Te Feng, father of Kao Te Fu, and lad who tried to
cut off his arm to save his mother's life. Suddenly, there was a knock at the door. Mr. Kao
opened it and there stood Mr. Yang. Kuo Shun
glanced up at him, "So you have returned," he said.
Mr. Yang ran across the room and threw himself on
the brick bed. Kuo Shun continued to recite the
mantra and instantly the man transformed into a
fox spirit and disappeared.

No one knows whether Mr. Yang was killed in
battle and then possessed by the fox or if he was
eaten by a wild fox who then assumed his form in
order to destroy Kuo Shun's cultivation. However,
because Kuo Shun cultivated the Great Compassion
Mantra and had a great deal of virtue, the fox was
forced to reveal its identity and disappear.

The following is an excerpt from an article
published in the *Hong Kong Hua Chiao Daily Newspaper*, da-
ted October 22, 1950:
"On the fifteenth day of the seventh lunar
month, 1944, the Master led his disciples before
the statue of the Buddha to burn incense and make
the following vow: 'If allowed to live a hundred
years, we will burn our bodies as an offering to
the Buddha in order to seek the supreme Buddha
Way.' In his mind, the Master bade Kuo Shun to do
the same, and at that moment Kuo Shun also vowed,
'I, disciple Kuo Shun, wish to imitate the sacrifice of Medicine Master Bodhisattva and burn my
entire body as an offering, but without waiting
until I am one hundred years old.'
"(At age thirty) Kuo Shun had obviously pene-
trated the secrets of dhyāna meditation, for on
the eighteenth day of the fourth lunar month, 1949,
saddened by the decline of Buddhism, the oppres-
sion of the Sangha and laity, the burning of sta-
tues and Sūtras, and in order to seek the supreme
enlightenment, he poured a quart and a half of oil
on a hundred pounds of sawdust, sat atop it in
full lotus and set it ablaze..." Seeing his hut
in flames, the villagers came running to find him
sitting upright in the ashes. When they reached
out and touched him, his body crumbled into ashes,
completely cremated--except for his unburnt heart.

KUO TSO

Thirteen hundred miles from Three Conditions Temple, in Chia Mu Tzu, lived a child named P'an who had spiritual powers. When he was only five years old he was able to cure other peoples' illnesses, and people came from hundreds of miles around to receive his cure. Although he could cure other peoples' illnesses, he couldn't cure his own sickness which was caused by a demon obstacle, and everyone called him, "Little Demon Obstacle."

One night, when he was eleven years old, he had the same dream three times. In his dream, Maitreya Bodhisattva appeared and said, "Would you like to have your sickness cured?"

"Oh, yes!" said the boy.

"Then go to Three Conditions Temple at P'ing Fang Station in Harbin. Leave home under Dharma Master An Tz'u and your sickness will be cured."

Because he had the dream three times in one night, he thought there was probably something to it, and the next morning he set out on foot for Harbin. As the Japanese had just surrendered, the road was dangerous and the ground was covered with mines. The boy carried two hand grenades and slept in the fields beside the road. One night he awoke and found himself surrounded by a pack of ferocious wolf dogs. Not particularly frightened, he sat up and said, "Hey, dogs, are you hungry? Come here and I'll give you a couple of grenades to eat!"

It's not known whether the dogs were afraid of the grenades or afraid of the boy's Dharma protectors. In any case, they ran.

Early in the morning on the day the boy arrived, the Master said to his disciple Kuo Neng, "A child will come here to leave home. Don't chatter with him, but come to get me right away."

"Hmmm..." said Kuo Neng. He didn't know exactly what that meant. At noon, he went to the Master. "Teacher! Teacher!" he exclaimed, "he's here! He's come to leave home just like you said he would!"

The Master went into the lobby and spoke with the pale, thin child. "What are you doing here?" he asked.

"I dreamt a fat monk told me that if I left home under Master An Tz'u my sickness would be cured. In fact, that's the fat monk, right there!" he said, pointing at the statue of Maitreya in the hallway.

"I don't believe you," the Master said. "I
think you're cold and hungry. Someone probably
told you that if you left home, although you would
not eat well, you wouldn't starve, and although
you wouldn't have fine clothes, you wouldn't freeze.
Isn't that the case? And so you made up the story
about Maitreya Bodhisattva."

The child denied it. The Master walked over
to the lunch table, took a bite of roll, chewed it
well, and spit it on the floor. "You say you want
to leave home," he said. "Eat that, and then we
will talk."

The boy immediately scooped it up and swallowed it. "All right," said the Master, "you may
leave home," and he named him "Kuo Tso."

Kuo Tso worked hard. He sat in dhyāna meditation, studied the sūtras, and bowed to the Buddha. In less than six months, he opened his five
eyes and knew what people had done in their past
lives, what sicknesses they had, and what they were
thinking. Later, someone asked him a question a-
bout his own spiritual powers in relation to those
of his teacher. Kuo Tso answered the question
carelessly, and with that one incorrect statement,
his five eyes closed and his karmic obstacle sickness returned.

In order to cure Kuo Tso's illness, the Master battled with sea monsters for weeks, day and
night, until the demon obstacle finally retreated.
The child's eyes, however, never opened again. The
sea monsters were enraged at having lost one of
their potential retinue and were determined to take
revenge.

One day the Master and his disciples were visiting a man named Kuo in the village of Tung Ching,
"east well" which was so-named because it lay in
a hollow surrounded by embankments on all four
sides, like a well. Suddenly it started to rain,
and a flash flood quickly swept through the town.
The water level reached as high as ten feet. Men,
women, and children, over forty in all, were drowned
in their homes, were trapped atop the brick beds,
or were swept away in the surge of high water.
Over eight hundred homes were destroyed.

Seeing the danger, the Master and his disciples began to recite the Great Compassion Mantra.
The flood raged outside the eight-foot fence made
of loosely-tied planks. The planks protected them,
and only a bit of water leaked in under the fence,

soaking the grass with no more than a few inches
of water.

     No one knew that the flood had been intended
solely to drown the Master, but many people said
they saw hundreds of strange "cow-like" creatures
jumping wildly in the water.

     The Master received the aid of the Buddhas
and Bodhisattvas, and the aid of the gods and dragons as well. But that was not the last time the
monsters would try to take revenge. He was to
meet them again, as we shall see, on the boat from
Tientsin to Hu Pei. So it is dangerous to cure
illnesses, for it often brings down the wrath of
ghosts and demons who will occasionally even assume
human form in order to take revenge.

WITH THE ELDER ABBOT CH'ANG JEN

     After the Elder Master Ch'ang Jen, Abbot of
Three Conditions Temple, had received the Dharma
transmission, he decided to build a monastery to
house the Sangha from the ten directions. One
wealthy merchant wished to give the large sum of
money needed, but the Abbot Ch'ang Jen put him off
agreeably, saying that since the Sangha from the
ten directions would use the building, there must
be donors from the ten directions to plant the
seeds of future blessings. He announced that he
would beg from every dwelling in the area. The
Master accompanied the Elder Abbot on his begging
rounds.

     In Tung Ching Tso village a family named Chang
raised fierce dogs which everyone feared. No one
dared visit them, but when the elder Abbot and the
Master reached the Chang's door, the dogs, to everyone's surprise, wagged their tails by way of greeting.

     One time they visited the home of Wu Wen Hui
in the Wu family village, and resting there they
discussed the amount they had collected. It was
a lot, and the Elder Abbot became rather conceited
about it, saying that it was the fame of the Filial Son Wong (he himself) that had been the major
influence, and the fact that people were heaping
money on them had no other cause.

     From that moment the Master said not one word,
thus showing his displeasure. At eight the next

morning they went out to visit the village elders,
more than ten in all, as well as some others. At
eleven in the morning they returned to the Wu's
for lunch. The money was counted--twenty-four
dollars, the smallest amount recorded to date.
The Master laughed and said, "Now, Abbot, where is
the fame of the Filial Son?"

The Elder Abbot replied, "Don't remain silent.
What I said was wrong. The many donations were
the result of the light of your reputation. I
hope that we can again work hard together."

The Master agreed.

***

On another occasion, they encountered a carpenter named Chang to whom the Master said, "You
should help with a donation of ten days' work on
the new monastery. OK?"

The carpenter agreed, but still reluctant, he
said that the long distance between the building
site and his home would greatly reduce his time
on the job. The Master replied by asking, "What
is your daily wage?"

"Twelve dollars," replied Chang.

"Then it will be enough," said the Master,
"for you to donate four days' wages." When Chang
protested that he didn't have it the Master said,
"It's in your pocket," and so it was, exactly forty eight dollars, and not a penny off. The carpenter could not ignore the strangeness of the
Master's reply and gladly became a donor.

***

Chinese mothers, according to the custom, like
to hear auspicious predictions, and many women with
young children brought them to the Elder Abbot to
ask if the child would grow up well. The Abbot
gave a pat reply, always in the affirmative. One
day the Master overheard the usual conversation
between an eager mother and the Abbot and afterwards asked him privately, "Abbot, do you really
know that all these children will be easily raised?
Why do you say to all their mothers that they will
be brought up easily?"

"That's what the mothers like to hear," he
replied.

"Yes," the Master said, "but on one occasion the child died within three days after you told the mother it would have a smooth childhood."

"What is an appropriate answer?" asked the Abbot.

"The next time you are asked," said the Master, "pass the question on to me and you'll see."

After a few days a young mother came in with her child and asked if it would grow up well. The Master replied, "If you want an answer, you must ask yourself. If your child, for example, originally was to have a long and fruitful life, but you led a debauched life, your deeds might very well shorten the child's life, or at least alter it drastically. If I were to give you a good prediction, it would be unrealized. On the other hand, if the child were to have a short life and I told you so, but then you constantly examined your conduct and changed yourself for the good, doing all kinds of meritorious deeds, the child's lifespan would increase, and you would say my words were worthless. Look for the answer in yourself; do not search outside."

While traveling through Harbin they met a foreign priest, a Catholic, who said, "What benefit could the Buddhists' superstitious practice of bowing before idols possibly have?"

"What benefit do you get by not bowing?" the Master replied.

"We aren't superstitious," he said.

"The Buddhist practice of bowing to the Buddha," said the Master, "strikes at the root of pride, arrogance, and feelings of self-importance. And it is good exercise. What could be more beneficial?"

"Superstition--confused belief--is a common occurrence," the Master continued. "The real problem lies not with confused belief but with the belief in the confused. Superstitious believers are common people, and even though they are confused, they can still wish to have faith in the upright Dharma, and in the future they will become Buddhas. Although people of other religions have faith, it is directed toward something that is confused, and the blind lead the blind into a false path. Confused and unawakened people do things the retribution for which is extremely painful; although they try to escape, they can't find a way out.

"Another group, those who are confused and have no belief, are heavenly demons who have fallen into the retinue of a demon king and actively disbelieve the true Dharma. Their suffering is even more extreme.

"Then there are those who have faith and are not confused, sages who become enlightened because of their belief in the proper Dharma. The steady light of Prajna shines, breaking the darkest confusion until they reach the unsurpassed result."

***

Although Japan had surrendered, the difficulties of the Chinese people were not yet over. The Russians, who were notorious for their ability to perpetrate every atrocity, invaded Manchuria.

When the Elder Abbot and the Master returned to three Conditions Temple, the Abbot carried more than a million dollars with him. On the way they were stopped to be searched by Russian soldiers. The Abbot placed his palms together and recited "Namo Amitabha Buddha" over and over again. The soldiers didn't touch him, and they arrived at their destination without further incident. Nonetheless the Master said, "The times are too chaotic; we should wait."

The elder Abbot replied, "No."

Thereupon the Master no longer continued to raise funds, but roamed about teaching those who had an affinity with him.

Here is the original newspaper account of how Disciple Kuo Shun burned himself as an offering to the Buddha. See page 61 for the English translation of this article.

宗教雙週刊　　一九五〇年十月廿二日

果舜大師

焚身供佛

東北哈陽鎮，距二十餘里，大員塢屯，龍□子盜，住持果舜大師，吉林□人，未出家前向以農爲業，日治時代彼派罷工，衣食不足，大盼其苦，每欲俊陳而逃，夜夢長窯柒人，腦不可妄動，待晉宿嚇，波之白狗。果舜彼嘗，後老人復來示夢，令其遁逃，并謂須跟隨頂於眼之白狗，由狗引時，則可安然渡過險關，果舜驚夢索助之，果見白犬一頭，投陰之出定，逃出鼠網，安然返家，精進用功，日中一食，脇不霑席，每入定，能一晝夜，舉凡一切過去，現在未來因果等事，止靜時故不知之，攄有關方面沈聞，心中作觀，令其所居之爭遂相隔二十餘里，蹑值共師有事指示，念而至。又於髮出家，投雙城縣三緣寺體上睡下輪法師爲師，精進用功，苦惱發顯，觸勸宿願，發無上心，願即燒身，以殉菩提，於是備辦豆三斤牛，木杵百斤，堆於佛前，將油倒於木杵上，結跏趺坐，服火焚，翌日鄉人見其葦蓬，有餘燼綠繞，近前觀之，始知大師坐焚，求無上道，令果舜亦燃，心中作觀，發願，彼正作中，彼即知民三十三年七月十五日，其師率衆弟子，於佛前燃未殼顯云，若能活於佛前燃香燒頂五，弟子果舜遇相當機會，顯教獎王菩薩，亦照模向佛前燃香燒頂五，生燒全身供佛，不待百歲也，諸如此類之事跡不勝其殼，由此足徵師，深入禪定三昧，果乳大師又於民三十八年夏，四月十八日，以佛教藝徵，僧徒大悲摧毀，殿像焚經，種種不堪言狀，目不忍覩，呼，大師以教難而自焚殉身，求無上道，末法期間，猶有如此所獻進之高僧，爲佛教而犧牲，光發極矣，證佛教徒個個长能抱此大無精神，向前邁進，何患佛法不興哉。

> *When the Venerable Master Hsüan Hua met the Venerable Master Hsü Yün, Master Yün asked him to take a position as instructor at the Nan Hua Vinaya Academy. The Master later took a position as head of the academy. Here is Master Yün's letter, exhorting Master Hua to remain at his post. See page 54.*

盧雲老和尚挽留度公之函。

To the Wise Attention of Dharma Master An Tz'u,

I have received your letter and read it carefully. You write too modestly. In truth, last year the Vinaya Academy relied upon you for the majority of its aid. I hope that from now on we can depend upon your assistance. Please don't even think of going elsewhere. I hope that you will decide to stay permanently to support and protect the Academy. That's my most earnest wish; I have nothing else to say except,

Best wishes, peace, and wisdom,

The Rag-robed Hsü Yün
Places his palms together

6th day of the 2nd lunar month, 1948

Also, if you don't wish to stay at Nan Hua, please come to Yün Men. The world is not a good place to be running around in at present.

The Master had long admired the great virtue of the Venerable Master Hsu Yun and had wished to journey to Nan Hua Monastery in Canton to meet him. In the autumn of 1946, after the surrender of the Japanese, travel once again became possible and the Master set out with his two disciples Kuo Neng and Kuo Shun. He left them at Prajñā Temple in Ch'ang Ch'un where they received the complete precepts, and he continued alone on his way to P'u T'o Mountain to receive the precepts there. He carried no possessions whatever and times were hard. He was often without even the money to buy a glass of water.

The Master stopped at Tientsin and stayed at the Great Compassion Academy where he attended Dharma Master T'an Hsu's lectures on the *Surāṅgama Sūtra*. He had wished to meet both Masters Tan Hsu and Ting Hsi, who was then called Ju Kuang. But it's not easy to meet the Elder Dharma Masters. First an appointment must be made with the guest prefect after which one might have to wait for days on end and still never have an interview.

Why did the Master wish to meet the two Dharma Masters? As a matter of principle, the Master draws near to all good knowing advisors. Master T'an Hsu was a famous teacher from the northeast, and the Master was at that time only a novice. He waited for several days, but no opportunity arose.

Then, on the day when Dharma Master Ting Hsi was planning to return to the northeast, the Master rose early in the morning and waited in the courtyard to have a few words with him. When he arrived, the Master bowed and introduced himself and said that he was planning to go to P'u T'o Mountain to receive the precepts.

"Don't involve me with your problems," said Ting Hsi. "Take them up with the Abbot. I don't

pay attention to such matters." Dharma Master
Ting Hsi thought that the Master had come to beg
for money but that certainly was not the case.
     "You're mistaken," said the Master. "I'm not
out to beg from you."
     "Oh?" said Dharma Master Ting Hsi. "Well
then there's even less of a problem!" and he left.
     The Master then met Dharma Master T'i Ching
and together with twelve others they boarded a
boat for Shanghai. In memory of the event which
followed, the Master has written a verse. It appears with a commentary, below:
     The verse:

> *Traveling by boat from Tientsin to Hu Pei during
> the autumn of 1946 and almost encountering disaster
> by shipwreck, a response was received and so the
> "Vomit Verse" was written:*
> *The Sāngha, fourteen in all, sailed south--*
>   *Long-bearded Elder, Srāmaṇera, green.*
> *The azure sea reached the sky--*
>   *sky for ten thousand miles;*
> *Black waves followed, billowing*
>   *wave upon wave a thousandfold.*
> *The Dharma subdued the monsters,*
>   *the boat was not capsized.*
> *The Wheel received the sages' aid*
>   *and vomiting was quelled.*
> *Happily reaching Hu Hai, hunger*
>   *and thirst were dispelled,*
> *At Wu Tsang, Right Enlightenment,*
>   *the sound of the jeweled conch.*

     The Sāngha, fourteen in all, sailed south. Dharma
Master T'i Ching led the group of fourteen monks.
He told them all to hand over their money to him
as that was his policy. The fourteen included
Bhikṣus Chih Hai, then called Mo Ju, T'i Ching,
Sheng Chao, Sheng Miao, Yung Ling, Ching Chieh,
Pen Chih, Ying Hsiu, Chiao Chih, Jen Hui, Chao
Ting, Hui Ju, Yen Hsiu, and the Master.
     Four of the group, Sheng Chao, Sheng Miao,
Ching Chieh, and the Master were young Srāmaṇeras,
novices, and so the verse says,
     Long bearded Elder, Srāmaṇera, green. Master T'i
Ching had a very long beard. He was also a strict
disciplinarian and liked to scold people more than
anything else. As soon as he saw someone he would
shut his eyes and bellow: "You, La La La!" The

Master also called him a long-bearded Elder because in northeast China they call robbers "red
beards" and, after all, Master T'i Ching did insist that all their money be turned over to him.

> *The azure sea reached the sky--*
> *sky for ten thousand miles.*
> *Black waves followed billowing--*
> *wave upon wave a thousandfold.*

The sea was calm when they first set out. After a while, however, it turned black, and the
waves rose to fifty, sixty, and seventy feet. The
boat, about three hundred feet long, was pitched
about violently like a toy. All one could do was
lie on the deck; it was impossible to stand up.
Usually the crossing was very easy, about a
one week trip. This time it took over two weeks
because there were thousands of sea monsters stir-
ring up the water in an attempt to drown the Master. Why did this happen?
You will remember that in northeast China the
Master had cured his disciple Kuo Tso of a disease
which was a major karmic obstacle and Kuo Tso had
later obtained some spiritual powers. Then, Kuo
Tso made an arrogant remark and lost his powers.
Shortly after that his sickness returned, more
fierce than before. At that time it was the Master's policy never to rest until he had cured his
disciples of their illnesses.
After three weeks of using the Sūrangama Mantra, Kuo Tso's demons fled. The Master met them
again at Tung Ching "east well" when they tried to
drown him in a flash flood. You see, curing illnesses often makes the demonic beings so angry
that they will stop at nothing in their thirst for
revenge. Now, the Master met them again and they
tried with all their might to capsize the boat and
drown him. They were extremely violent.
No one else was aware of the cause of the
storm. Everyone got sick. Only Master T'i Ching
manifested some "spiritual powers" by not throwing
up. The Master vomited bile which burned his lips.
He had no strength, no breath, and was on the
verge of death.
"Kuan Yin Bodhisattva," the Master said, "if
I can be of use in the world, then let me live.
If I am of no use in helping living beings, then
I'll die. It's no problem." It was at that point

that the Master truly understood the meaning of
the remark he often makes today, that is, "Everything's O.K." He had put his life in the hands of
the Buddhas and Bodhisattvas.

*The Wheel received the sages' aid and vomiting was
quelled*. As it turned out, there were certain methods, dharmas, the Master employed to subdue the
sea monsters and so the boat was not capsized.
The "Wheel" might refer to the steamship, literal-
ly "wheel boat" in Chinese, because the Buddhas
and Bodhisattvas secretly helped out and prevented
the boat from turning over. Or you could say it
refers to the Master, whose name includes the word
"Wheel."

Since the one-week trip had stretched into
two and was going on three, the food was rationed
and no one ate his fill. Everyone was hungry.
When one of them complained, Master T'i Ching scolded him. "You, La La La!" he shouted, "all you
do is talk about being hungry!" and he pointed at
the Master and said, "Look at Master An Tz'u. He
only eats one meal a day and he never complains."

Master Yung Ling said, "Of course he doesn't.
He eats on the sly. He sneaks the rice crust."

Why did he say that? One day the cook had
given the Master a small bit of rice crust which
the Master didn't eat but passed on to the little novice, Sheng Miao. When Master Yung Ling saw the
Master take the crust he assumed the Master ate
it and so he slandered the Master to everyone he
saw.

And so it was that for almost two weeks no
one ate his fill. It didn't really matter, however, because regardless of what one ate, it was
puked right back up, with bitter stomach fluids.

Happily reaching Hu Hai, hunger and thirst dispelled.
When the voyage had become totally unbearable,
they arrived, finally, in Shanghai, also called
Hu Hai, and T'i Ching said, "Buy noodles!"

They made more noodles than they could eat
and as they were about to dump the leftovers into
the sea, Master Yung Ling said to the Master, "Do
you want some?"

The Master thought, "For the last two weeks
they didn't have enough food and now they are
throwing it away. That's too pitiful!" And so
he drank two bowls of the water the noodles were
cooked in.

Master Yung Ling went running to Master T'i
Ching. "He claims he doesn't eat," he said, "but
when you're not looking he will eat anything!"

Long-bearded T'i Ching looked at the Master
for a long time, "How could you eat the soup?" he
said. "You claim not to eat in the morning and
then you steal food." He scolded the Master se-
verely, but the Master didn't defend himself.

At *Wu Tsang, Right Enlightenment, the sound of the
jeweled conch.* Wu Tsang is Hu Pei Province and
Right Enlightenment is the name of the temple where
the Master stayed. He slept on a meditation bench
by the door, without a sleeping bag or blanket,
and wore the same clothes day and night. Everyone
said, "How come you're not cold?"

"Who is cold?" the Master answered, pretend-
ing to be very stupid. Later, many said, "Ah,
your bitter practices are something we could never
bear."

Long bearded T'i Ching never did return the
Master's money, by the way.

At Right Enlightenment Temple, the Master
served as a verger. Although the winters were
bitter, he continued to wear only the same three
layers of cotton clothing. He sat on a straw mat
and watched the door and made great progress in
his meditation. The whole time he was there a
rare fragrance filled the hall--a fragrance not of
this world.

The Master had no friends in Hu Pei. From
morning to night no one paid any attention to him
and many looked down on him as a useless rice-
monk. Nonetheless, the Master was always extremely respectful towards everyone. He practiced aus-
terities, working as the cook, water-carrier, and
janitor. While cleaning out the pit toilets the
Master came to understand that jealousy and lazi-
ness are the karmic conditions which lead to rebirth as a dung-beetle. Pit toilets stink to high
heaven, but the worms that live in them think they
are quite comfortable.

In 1947 the Master again set out for P'u T'o
Mountain, the pilgrimage site sacred to Kuan Yin
Bodhisattva, and received the ordination. Afterwards, he went to Su Chou, to Ling Yen Temple, and
undertoook an intensive study of the Buddhist ca-
non and teaching schools. In the fall, he went on
to K'ung Ch'ing Mountain to attend a ten week medi-

tation session and pass the winter. There he met
the Masters Liao Ch'eng and Ming Kuan.

     During that period many cultivators attended
the week-long sessions, but only the Master and
the old bearded Ming Kuan spent the entire seventy
days in the Ch'an Hall. When the others retired
to their rooms to sleep, the two cultivators sat
on through the night.

     Liao Ch'eng was the Abbot of K'ung Ch'ing,
and occasionally the Master talked with him, Ming
Kuan, and the others. The Master's banter left
them all speechless. "Old Ch'an Sitter," the Master once inquired of an old-timer in the politest
of tones, "Superior One," he continued with utmost
courtesy before demanding abruptly, "HOW COME YOU
CAN'T SIT!"

     "I'm too old," came the defensive reply. "My
legs are stiff, my back is bent, and my teeth hurt.
I can't do it anymore. I'm not as young as I used
to be."

     "Your teeth hurt?" said the Master. "How is
it that teeth can hurt? Think it over, is it your
teeth which hurt or is it you who hurt? If it is
your teeth which hurt, they can't talk; how can
you speak for them? If it is you who hurt, why do
you say it is your teeth?"

     The cultivator was dumbfounded. He didn't
know if his teeth hurt or if he himself hurt. The
Master was so skilled at delivering such verbal
blows and in enduring the rigors of the repeated
Ch'an sessions that many claimed the Master had
been enlightened during the ten-week session at
K'ung Ch'ing. In fact, later, when the Master was
in Hong Kong, Liao Ch'eng went to Canton province
to beg and used the light of the Master's reputation to drum up business. "The Venerable Master
became enlightened at my temple, you know," he
would say, "and I certified him." Blatantly clai-
ming to be the Master's good knowing advisor, he
implied that he himself was enlightened and could
certify an enlightenment. There are all kinds of
people in the world.

     In the first month of the Chinese New Year,
1948, the Master returned to Shanghai, preparing
to take a boat for Hang Chou. At Kuan Yin Ku Ch'a
in Shanghai, the Master met Dharma Master Ju Lien.
Ju Lien looked the Master up and down and said,
"You're a new preceptee. According to the rules,
we can't allow you to stay here."

"Then throw your crutch over the side."

"But I can't walk without it!" said the cripple.

"I'm trying to help you," said the Master. "Do you think I'd cheat you?"

The cripple tossed his crutch over the side. The Master rubbed the cripple's legs for about fifteen minutes and recited the Great Compassion Mantra. "Stand up," he said to the cripple, and the cripple stood upright. "Walk," he said, and the cripple began to walk. "Now, run!" said the Master, and the cripple ran around the Master in circles, overjoyed.

Seeing this, all the passengers rushed at the Master. "My arm hurts," said one. "Won't you heal my back?" said another. Fifty or sixty people gave him money, asking for his help.

"Are you afraid of being beaten?" was his reply to their requests.

One man had an infected leg. The Master kicked him smartly in the shins and asked, "How do you feel?"

"Why, I'm completely well," he said, amazed. Another had a sore arm. The Master punched him and he had no more pain. So it was that they all came to the Master and were socked, kicked, and punched out of their various illnesses.

Then the passengers all crowded around him seeking to make appointments for their relatives and friends. "My sister has been sick in Nanking for years, could you..." The Master spoke expediently to them all. "Yes, yes," he said, "I'll certainly go." When the boat docked, however, he hurried down the side gang plank and slipped away from them all.

He had received about $800,000 in national currency, 200,000 of which he used to buy a train ticket. At the train station he met Dharma Master Chou I. "Where are you going?" the Master asked him.

"To Canton," squeaked Master Chou I in his Hu Pei accent, "to see the Venerable Master Hsu Lau."

"Do you have the train fare?" the Master asked.

"No," he said, "but we'll just wait and see what happens." He meant he was going to hop a train.

The Master bought him a ticket, and the two of them boarded the train. The Master himself

"I may be a new preceptee," said the Master, "but where did all you old preceptees come from?"

"All right," said Ju Lien, "you can stay."

The next day they had a chat. The Master had written a lot of poetry, and he showed his poems to Master Ju Lien, who sighed in praise, "Ah, these poems!" he said. Then he advised the Master to give up writing poetry. "If you're attached to the marks of language," he said, "you cannot obtain liberation."

"But has the High Master obtained liberation?" the Master asked.

"No, but I intend to go ahead and practice the Way," he answered.

"Right!" said the Master, and he stopped writing poems. Later, when the Master announced that he was leaving Master Ju Lien said, "Please stay for a few more days."

"No," said the Master, "I really can't. I'm a new preceptee and you are all old preceptees..."

ARE YOU AFRAID OF BEING BEATEN?

In Shanghai the Master boarded a boat for Hang Chou on his way to Canton, by way of Pao T'ung Monastery in Hu Pei. The steamship gave free passage to members of the Saṅgha as they lent an auspicious air to the journey; there were rarely storms or other difficulties when Saṅgha members were on board.

On board the Master saw a cripple and the moment he saw him he knew that he could cure his illness. He also knew it would cause a lot of trouble if he cured it right away and so he waited until about eight o'clock in the morning on the day they were to reach Hang Chou and then he asked the cripple, "Why do you walk like that?"

The man said that he had been imprisoned as a black market charcoal dealer and the cold, damp cell had given him severe arthritis. His bones were so deformed that he had to walk with a cane, crouched over like a duck.

At that time it was the Master's policy to work untiringly to cure illnesses to the extent that he would have given up his own life in order to save another. "Would you like to get better?" he asked.

"Of course," said the cripple.

would not have spent more than 50,000 in national
currency for food, but Dharma Master Chou I had
to have something at every stop. Finally, when
he asked for some rice gruel, the Master just
reached in his pocket, pulled out the money and
handed it to Master Chou I. "Here," he said, "take
it all. I don't want to be bothered with it anymore," and from then on he didn't handle money.

PART VIII: THE DHARMA TRANSMISSION

    Arriving in Canton after three thousand miles
of travel, the Master went to Nan Hua Monastery
and bowed before the Venerable Master Hsu Yun who
was then 109 years old. The two masters chatted
and the Venerable Hsu Yun recognized the Master to
be a vessel worthy of the propagation of the Dharma, sealed and certified his spiritual skill, and
transmitted the wonderful mind-to-mind seal of all
the Buddhas to the Master. Thus the Master became
the Forty-fifth Patriarch from Sākyamuni Buddha,
the Eighteenth Patriarch in China from Bodhidharma,
and the Ninth Patriarch of the Wei Yang Lineage.
Of their meeting, the Master has written:

> *The Noble Yun saw me and said, "Thus it is."*
> *I saw the Noble Yun and verified, "Thus it is."*
> *The Noble Yun and I, both Thus,*
> *Hoped that every living being*
> *In the Universe would be Thus too.*

    The Venerable Master Hsu Yun then asked the
Master to be an instructor in the Nan Hua Vinaya
Academy. The Master refused. "Your student has
come ten thousand miles to meet the Good Knowing
One," said the Master. "If the Venerable Master
can guarantee that I will be able to end birth and
death, then I'll gladly jump into a cauldron of
boiling soup, walk on fire, give up my body and
bones, accept the position you offer and not resign."
    The Master Hsu Yun replied, "One eats one's
own food to fill oneself; one ends one's own birth
and death. If I were to say that I guaranteed that
you will end birth and death I'd be cheating you.
I don't do that sort of thing. In cultivation,
one should concentrate on inner skill and outer
accomplishment. One should not be an independent
Arhat, looking only after his own good. One should
practice the Bodhisattva way for the good of all,

support the Triple Jewel, and be of service to
everyone. In that way, one may perfect blessings
and virtue and quite naturally end birth and death."
     The Master again refused to take the position.
Master Hsu Yun continued his exhortations. "You
came all the way from northeast China to meet me.
If you are not going to obey my instructions, why
did you bother to come at all?"
     The Master accepted.

     The Master observed the words and actions of
the Venerable Master Hsu Yun and found them to be
of extraordinarily pure virtue. The Venerable Master constantly acted as a model and guide, willing-
ly taking upon himself the bitterness of the hard
work of propagating the Dharma.

TEACHING THE DHARMA TO BENEFIT ALL

     During the spring precept-transmission in
1948 the Master one day heard the loud roar of a
tiger not far away. His Dharma friends told him,
"The tiger is the Venerable Master's disciple. It
lives in a cave behind the mountain and always
comes out to protect the precept ceremonies. When
the ceremonies are over it returns to its cave."

     In the fifth month, after the transmission
of the precepts, the Master was serving as verger
in the altar room of the Fifth Patriarch at Nan
Hua Monastery. At that time a layman named Huang
Chu Tsai came to visit. Upon first seeing the
Master, Layman Huang felt a strong affinity with
him and invited him to Kiangsi in the district of
Nan Ch'eng to lecture on the *Amitābha Sūtra*. They
fixed the date for the tenth day of the sixth
month, but the Master was detained on the road.
     Meanwhile, the assembly had gathered at the
temple in Chiang Hsi and was on the one hand bowing to the Buddha and on the other watching hope-
fully for the Master. Layman Huang consulted the
Kuan Yin divination stalks daily, asking Kuan Yin
Bodhisattva when the Master would arrive.
     Suddenly while reciting the Buddha's name, the
the wisdom of a laywoman named Hsiang unfolded and
she said, "The Dharma Master won't come during
this recitation week. We should arrange for another recitation week during which we should be

mindful of Earth Store Bodhisattva." Then she named the day of the Master's arrival.

The Master arrived on the designated day during the Earth Store Bodhisattva Recitation Session, and everyone thought the laywoman had become enlightened.

In the first week of the seventh month, the Master began lecturing to a group of more than a hundred people. Among them was a layman named Kuo Le, who had been plagued by a demonic illness for over ten years. Since something prevented him from being able to worship, he knew his illness was caused by a demon. He had sought the aid of Buddhist and Taoist masters who cultivated such dharmas as the Great Compassion Repentance, the Liang Huang Pao Repentance and the ceremony for releasing dead souls, and he also recited Sūtras, but nothing was effective. When the old man heard the Master speak the *Amitābha Sūtra*, however, his demon fled in terror, and the man recovered his normal senses and was never again bothered by it.

Another member of the assembly, a young girl named Hsu whose body was half-paralyzed, was completely healed after hearing the Sūtra. The Master's following increased greatly as many, many people took refuge with the Master.

NOTES ON THE PURE LAND

As a child, the Master most liked to bow to the Buddha and recite the Buddha's name. Accordingly, he has written this verse in praise of recitation.

> *If you recite the Buddha's name*
> *   recite it without cease.*
> *The mouth recites "Amita"*
> *   and makes a unity.*
> *False thoughts do not arise;*
> *   samādhi is attained.*
> *For birth in the Pure Land*
> *   your hope is not in vain.*
>
> *If you always feel aversion for*
> *   the suffering sahā world,*
> *Then be rid of the red-dust thoughts*
> *   within your mind.*

> *Seek rebirth in Ultimate Bliss*
> *with serious intent*
> *By putting down defiled thoughts*
> *and returning to the pure.*

The Master delivered the following instruction during a seven-day recitation session in Kiangsi:

"The Dharma-door of reciting the Buddha's name is also called the Pure Land Dharma-door. By means of this method all can enter the Pure Land, for it receives those of all three dispositions and gathers the intelligent and deluded. Wise people with superior wisdom, average people with ordinary intelligence, and inferior, deluded people--those of all three dispositions need only recite the name and they will be reborn in the Pure Land. Thus it is the convenient means within the convenient means, the short cut among short cuts, and is most suited to beings in the Dharma-ending age.

"If one is simply able to recite 'Namo Amitābha Buddha,' one will certainly be reborn in the Land of Ultimate Bliss, where, transformationally born from a lotus, one will see the Buddha and awaken to the patience of the uncreated, never again to retreat to the Small Vehicle or to the status of a common person. If what I say is not so, I will gladly descend into the hells.

"Yesterday someone asked me, 'When I recite the Buddha's name, I have too much idle thinking. How can I stop it?'

"Pay no attention to how much idle thinking you are doing. Just keep reciting the Buddha's name with all your heart. There is a common saying,

> *When the clear-water pearl*
> *is thrown in muddy water,*
> *the muddy water turns clear.*
>
> *When the Buddha's name*
> *enters the deluded mind,*
> *the deluded mind becomes the Buddha.*

"Recitation itself is the cure for idle thinking. Why add a head on top of your head by looking for another method?"

BANDITS

In the eighth month, after the lecture series, the Master returned to Nan Hua Monastery. In the ninth month, he met with a gang of bandits who were intent on ransacking the monastery.

One evening, the Master heard bandits beating on the monastery door. "Open up!" they shouted. "This is the government!" The Master refused to let them in.

Two of the Master's disciples who were very young had hidden under the bed in the next room. The Master faced the thieves alone. When he finally opened the door, they ran in, swinging clubs and guns. They aimed their guns at the Master and said, "Why didn't you open the door?"

"You are thieves and bandits," the Master said. "You came to rob me, not to give me gifts. Think it over. If you had been in my place would you have opened the door for me?"

They continued to threaten the Master with their guns, but the Master was unmoved. "Give us your money!" they shouted. The Master, who was wearing the same thin, tattered robe that he had worn in northeast China while sitting beside his mother's grave, said to the thieves, "Look at my robe. Do I look like a rich man?"

"No..." they said, "but your students must have money."

"If the teacher is penniless, surely the students will be poorer yet," said the Master. Then, as the bandits ran through the monastery, the Master followed them closely, harassing them and ordering them not to steal things.

The following day at class, Dharma Master Huai Huai I announced to all, "In the monastery, only one man was not afraid of the thieves--Dharma Master Hsuan Hua."

"No, that's not correct," the Master quickly replied. "As far as I know, there were four people: the Great Master the Sixth Patriarch sat unmoved in bright samādhi; Master Han Shan was also unruffled. Master Tan T'ien was quite calm, although he had less concentration and stuck out his head to take a look around. These three great teachers all did far better than I. I had no concentration whatever. I just chased the bandits all

over the monastery ordering them not to steal anything.[1]
     When the Venerable Master Hsu Yun heard of
the bandits, he returned to Nan Hua from Yun Men
and called a general meeting. Since the students
were afraid and wanted to leave the monastery, the
Master agreed to take the position as head of the
Vinaya Academy until the first day of 1949, thus
dispelling their fears.

SUBDUING THE HUNDRED-SON POISONOUS SNAKE

     While at Nan Hua Monastery, the Master had a
great disciple who could cure illnesses. The disciple had studied the Dharma of the Forty-Two Hands
so thoroughly that his cures happened instanta-
neously. Although the Master had told him not to
pay attention to people's illnesses, still he liked
to do it occasionally. As a result he became possessed by an intractable hundred-son poisonous
snake.
     No one could even catch the disciple. He
would slither around and if anyone got near him
he would slip by him so quickly that no one could
catch him. Only the Master was able to catch him,
and that was because he used a special method. But
at first, even the Master couldn't subdue the demon. After trying various mantras and dharmas he
realized he couldn't handle it alone.
     The hundred-son snake spit venom. If a lit-
tle landed on your skin you would get sick and if
a lot got on your skin you would go crazy. The
snake was a descendant of the poisonous dragon
which the Sixth Patriarch subdued at Nan Hua Monastery some 1200 years before. It would invariably possess someone during every precept transmission ceremony held at Nan Hua Monastery and cause
him to go berserk. None of the Dharma Masters
could handle it, and if the Master hadn't gone to
Nan Hua, it would still be giving them trouble.
Most people, however, knew nothing about it.

---

[1]The gilded, undecaying bodies of the Sixth Patriarch, Master Han Shan, and Master Tan T'ien are
preserved for veneration at Nan Hua Monastery. The
body of Master Tan T'ien leans slightly forward.

Six months after the Master's disciple became possessed by the snake, the Master met an old cultivator who could enter samādhi and had some spiritual skill. He had left home when he was eight and had attended eight ninety-day sessions during which he constantly walked and never slept. As a result, his spiritual skill was such that he was able to help the Master subdue the snake demon. The cultivator would enter samādhi while the Master employed a dharma and then the Master would enter samādhi while the old cultivator used a dharma. They conquered the snake, finally, and trapped it in the jar, sealing the jar with a mantra under the condition that the snake cannot come out for five hundred years.

The Master has said, "Don't sell your cultivation. I never tell people to take refuge with me and I don't encourage people to believe in me. If you are a good person, people can tell just by looking at you; what is the use of advertising yourself? That's simply too stupid. When anyone tries to sell his cultivation to me, I reply with the following, 'You work so hard, surely you're a Bodhisattva. Personally, I'm a karmic obstacle ghost, because whenever I do the tiniest bit of good, I feel compelled to brag about it to everyone I meet. Now you know.'
"See? Instead of criticizing them, I criticize myself."

***

As leader of the assembly at Nan Hua Monastery, the Master held the highest position in the general assembly of students. Everyday he went into the "clouds and water hall" to chat with the newly arrived monks and he bowed to them all. The next morning, at recitation, when they saw the Master standing in the first position in the front row, they felt quite surprised and a little embarrassed.
Whenever someone left Nan Hua Monastery, the Master would carry his pack and escort him down the road at least as far as the monastery gate. While he was on the road, he was often so poor that he couldn't afford a cup of tea, and generally, no one paid any attention to him as a newcomer. Knowing the hardships involved, the Master

made a special point of welcoming new people. What
advantages did the practice have? None at all.

MEDITATION INSTRUCTION DELIVERED
AT NAN HUA MONASTERY

The Master said, "All of you good knowing advisors of great virtue: The Dharma-door of the
mind-ground is spoken of as the most supreme and
high, but truly to be able to certify and gain liberation is not an easy matter. As I personally
have not deeply investigated it, I can only speak
casually with you and can't reveal the essentials.
"First of all, when one investigates dhyāna
and seeks certification, one should not depart from
one's own mind. Only in that way can one attain
one's aim.
"Now, let us speak of the three non-outflow
studies: morality, concentration, and wisdom. It
would appear that in the Dhyāna School morality is
not stressed, for one simply sits in meditation
and then runs to exercise the body. There is no
conversation and no random thought. But as one
looks closely, he will see that in this way the
three karmic vehicles of body, mouth, and mind are
kept clear, pure, and free of offense. That could
be called the 'morality of non-morality.'
"With morality, the body becomes tranquil and
one attains concentration. At all times there is
equilibrium as a bright light gradually shines
forth and one's wisdom unfolds.
"The state of perfect morality, concentration, and wisdom is enlightenment. At that time
there is, inwardly, no 'self' and, outwardly, no
'other.' The mountains, rivers, and the great
earth with all the myriad appearances no longer
exist. All is empty; what was not empty is made
empty; what was not non-existent, no longer exists.
Still and clear, free and easy, one returns to the
origin. This moment cannot be captured in words
or reckoned in thought, for it is the state of the
inconceivable.
"All of you should relinquish your afflictions
and your thoughts of self and others. Drive your
arrogance, flattery,and falsehood completely away.
Look carefully into your meditation topic and ask
yourself, "Who is reciting the Buddha's name?"

Continue until the waters are fathomed and the
mountains scaled. Then take that one last step.
Let go of your hold on the cliff and you'll gain
a whole new life and spontaneously obtain liberation. At that time you will know that our past
Patriarchs were not wasting their breath. Understand? Then meditate!"

After acting as *ārāaya* at the 1949 transmission
of the precepts, the Master accompanied the Venerable Master Hsu Yun to Shao Kuan, to Ta Chien Monastery. When the Venerable Master Yun suggested
that he continue with him to Yun Men the Master
agreed to join him there, but insisted on first returning to Nan Hua.
On the first day of the fifth month, the Master arrived at Ta Chiao Monastery in Yun Men and
acted as leader of the assembly as he had at Nan
Hua. The Master became ill because of the damp-
ness of the weather and asked to return to Canton
to heal his illness. Although the Master promised
to return, the Venerable Master Hsu Yun only re-
luctantly gave his permission, fearing that he
would never see the Master again.
The Master traveled to Canton and then to Hong
Kong, arriving in Hong Kong in the seventh month
of 1949. He then went to Liu Jung Monastery in
Canton where Abbot Ming Kuan had planned to return
to Yun Men on the fifteenth day of the eighth month,
but at the beginning of the eight month the road
was cut off and so on the eighteenth day of the
eighth month he returned to Hong Kong.

FOREWARNED

While at Liu Jung Monastery, the Master missed
morning recitation one morning because he had a
headache. Even though the Master held one of the
three positions in the monastery in which one has
the privilege of not attending early recitation,
when Master Ming Kuan heard about the Master's ab-
sence he scolded the Master and accused him of la-
ziness.
Realizing that reasoning with the Abbot was
useless, the Master prepared to leave, even though
he didn't have a cent. "You can't go," Abbot Ming
Kuan cried. "What will I do without you?"

"You still have your long beard," said the
Master. "What's the problem?"

Before the Master left, however, he advised
Abbot Ming Kuan to take several steps immediately:
"You should do three things," he said. "First of
all, take all the temple money (there were barrels
of it destined for construction of a pagoda,) and
divide it among the Bhiksus in residence here.
Take half yourself, since you are the head, and
divide the other half among the Bhiksus. If they
want to live here, let them, but tell them that
they must buy their own food. And I don't want any
of the money.

"Secondly, go to Hong Kong and build a temple
which will be affiliated with this one. Thirdly,
take all the valuable Dharma objects with you to
Hong Kong. Don't leave any behind."

Hearing the Master's proposals, Dharma Master
Ming Kuan said, "But I'm afraid of the causes and
conditions. I'm afraid of the result..."

The Master took leave and went to the railway
station accompanied by his disciple Heng Ting who
had been residing there with him. When they arrived, a layman approached them with two tickets
which he had bought and decided not to use. He
gave them to the Master.

Meanwhile, Master Ming Kuan had sent a messenger to the station with $10.00 for the Master.
When the messenger reached the Master he stuffed
the money in the Master's pocket, only to watch
the Master throw it back out again on the floor.

The Master arrived in Hong Kong on the eighteenth day of the eighth month. Three days had
passed from the time he had given Master Ming Kuan
the instructions, but Master Ming Kuan had paid
them no heed. On the twenty-second, the People's
Army arrived in Canton and all money and property
were confiscated. Ming Kuan and the other Bhiksus
stuffed their suitcases full and headed for the
train station, but it was too late. Everything
was seized. And Master Ming Kuan had feared the
result!

Later he got out, but had nothing to bring
with him. He said to the Master with regret, "If
only I had believed you and done what you said..."

"You still have your long beard," replied the
Master. "What's the problem?"

The Master has said:

"You need only fear that you yourself will not
be true. Do not fear that others will surpass you.
I am never jealous of others and I pay no attention to whether or not they may be jealous of me.
Whether they envy me or not makes no difference,
I am happy all the same, for I am of one substance
with the Buddhas.
"If you would like to come along with me and
be of one substance with the nature of the Dharma
Realm, fine. If you don't, I don't care. When
you have arrived at that state, then you can speak
the Buddhadharma."

The Master has said:

"Anyone can become enlightened. Put down
whatever it is that you can't put down--and put it
down the hardest."

Publications from the Buddhist Text Translation Society

All BTTS translations include extensive inter-linear commentary by the Venerable Tripitaka Master Hsuan Hua unless otherwise noted. All works available in softcover only unless otherwise noted.
ISBN Prefix: 0-917512

SUTRAS (Scriptures spoken by the Buddha):

AMITABHA SUTRA - This Sutra, which was spoken by the Buddha without being formally requested as in other Sutras, explains the causes and circumstances for rebirth in the Land of Ultimate Bliss of Amitabha (Limitless Light) Buddha. The commentary contains extensive information on common Buddhist terminology, and stories on many of the Buddha's foremost disciples. 01-4, 204 pgs., $8. (Also available in Spanish. $8.)

DHARANI SUTRA - This Sutra tells of the past events in the life of the Bodhisattva of great compassion Avalokiteshvara (Kuan Yin), and the various ways of practicing the Great Compassion Mantra, and its many benefits. It is a fundamental Secret School method. The second half of the publication is divided up into three sections. The first explains the meaning of the mantra line by line. The second has Chinese poems and drawings of division bodies of Kuan Yin for each of the 84 lines of the mantra. The last section contains drawings and verses in English on each of the 42 Hands and Eyes of Kuan Yin. This is the first English translation of this scripture.
13-8, 352 pgs., $12.

千手千眼大悲心陀羅尼經, all of the material noted above for the DHARANI SUTRA, except the commentary and the section explaining the meaning of the mantra. All the material is in Chinese only. 210 p., $6.00.

DHARMA FLOWER (LOTUS) SUTRA - In this Sutra, which was spoken in the last period of the Buddha's teaching, the Buddha proclaims the ultimate principles of the Dharma which unites all previous teachings into one. When completed the entire Sutra will be from 15 to 20 volumes. The following are those volumes which have been published to date:

VOL. I, INTRODUCTION. Discusses the Five Periods and
Eight Teachings of the T'ien T'ai School and then
analyzes the School's Fivefold Profound Meanings as
they relate to the Sutra. The last portion intro-
duces Tripitaka Master Kumarajiva, who translated
the Sutra from Sanskrit to Chinese. 85 p., 16-2,$3.95.

VOL. II, INTRODUCTION, CHAPTER ONE. This describes
the setting for the speaking of the Sutra, which includes the nature of the assembly who gathered to
hear it, the Buddha's emitting of light, the questioning of Maitreya Bodhisattva, and the response
from Maitreya Bodhisattva. 324 p., 22-7, $7.95.

VOL. III, EXPEDIENT METHODS, CHAPTER TWO. After the
Buddha emerges from samadhi he speaks. The Buddha's
foremost Arhat disciple in wisdom, Shariputra, requests the Buddha to speak further. After being requested three times the Buddha proclaims for the first
time that all living beings have the potential to
become Buddhas. 183 p., 26-X, $7.95.

VOL. IV, A PARABLE, CHAPTER THREE. The Buddha explains the nature of his teaching by means of an
analogy of an elder who tries to rescue his five hundred children who are absorbed in their play in a
burning house. 371 p., 62-6, $8.95.

VOL. V, BELIEF AND UNDERSTANDING, CHAPTER FOUR. Four
of the Buddha's foremost Arhat disciples tell a story
similar to the Bible's prodigal son, to express their
happiness upon hearing that they too could become
Buddhas in the future. 200 p., 64-2, $6.95.

*VOL. VI, MEDICINAL HERBS, CHAPTER FIVE, and CONFERRING
PREDICTIONS, CHAPTER SIX.* In these chapters the Buddha
uses the analogy of a rain-cloud to illustrate how his
teaching benefits all beings with total impartiality,
and he also predicts that the previously mentioned
Arhat disciples will become Buddhas in the future. In
bestowing his prediction he tells what their future
Buddha name will be, as well as the name of their world
system and kalpa, and the scope of their Dharma.
161 p., 65-0, $6.95.

*VOL. VII, PARABLE OF THE TRANSFORMATION CITY, CHAPTER
SEVEN.* In this volume the Buddha teaches that the at-

tainment of his Arhat disciples is like a transformation city which he conjured up as an expedient when
they became weary with the journey to becoming Buddhas.
250 p., $7.95.

*VOL. VIII, FIVE HUNDRED DISCIPLES RECEIVE PREDICTIONS,
CHAPTER EIGHT, and BESTOWING PREDICTIONS UPON THOSE
STUDYING AND BEYOND STUDY, CHAPTER NINE.* More than a
thousand followers receive predictions that they will
become Buddhas in the future. 160 p., 71-5, $6.95.

VOL. IX, THE DHARMA MASTER, CHAPTER TEN. This volume
is now in preparation and will be available soon.

Other volumes of the *DHARMA FLOWER SUTRA* forthcoming.

FLOWER ADORNMENT (AVATAMSAKA) SUTRA VERSE PREFACE
清涼國師 華嚴經序淺釋), a succinct verse commentary
by T'ang Dynasty National Master Ch'ing Liang (the
Master of seven emperors), which gives a complete over-
view of all the fundamental principles contained in the
Sutra in eloquent style. First English translation.
BI-LINGUAL EDITION Chinese & English. 244 p., 28-6, $7.00.

FLOWER ADORNMENT SUTRA PROLOGUE. A detailed explanation
of the principles of the Sutra utilizing the Hsien Shou
method of analyzing scriptures known as the Ten Doors,
by National Master Ch'ing Liang. Will be approximately
5 to 10 volumes upon completion. The following volumes
have been published to date:

*THE FIRST DOOR: THE CAUSES AND CONDITIONS FOR THE
ARISAL OF THE TEACHING.* 252 p., 66-9, $10.00.

*THE SECOND DOOR, PART ONE: THE STORES AND TEACHINGS
TO WHICH IT BELONGS.* 280 p., 73-1, $10.00.

THE SECOND DOOR, PART TWO, is now in preparation
and will be available soon.

Other volumes of the *PROLOGUE* are forthcoming.

清涼國師 華嚴經疏淺釋 , entirety of the *AVATAMSAKA
SUTRA PROLOGUE,* from First to Tenth Door, together with
interlinear commentary by Ven. Abbot Hua in four Volumes. CHINESE. $5.00, $8.50, $8.50, & $5.00.